CASES IN MANAGEMENT ACCOUNTING AND BUSINESS FINANCE

Published in 2006 by
The Institute of Chartered Accountants in Ireland
CA House, Pembroke Road
Ballsbridge, DUBLIN 4

Designed and typeset by Compuscript, Shannon, Ireland
Printed by Four Print, Dublin, Ireland

ISBN   0 903854 18 X

ISBN-13   978 0-903854 18 4

Copyright of publication rests in entirety with The Institute of Chartered Accountants in Ireland (ICAI). All rights reserved. No part of this text may be reproduced or transmitted in any form or by any means, including photocopying, Internet or e-mail dissemination, without the written permission of the ICAI. Such written permission must also be obtained before any part of this document is stored in a retrieval system of any nature.

The opinions expressed in this publication are those of the authors and editors and do not necessarily represent the views of the ICAI. The text is designed to provide accurate and authoritative information in regard to the subject matter covered. It is sold on the understanding that the ICAI is not engaged in rendering professional services. If professional advice or other expert assistance is required, the services of a competent professional should be sought.

© Cases in Management Accounting and Business Finance
The Institute of Chartered Accountants in Ireland, 2006

CASES IN MANAGEMENT ACCOUNTING AND BUSINESS FINANCE

Edited by Noel Hyndman and Donal McKillop

The Institute of Chartered Accountants in Ireland
Dublin

Contents

The management accounting cases are presented first (section A), followed by the cases in business finance (section B). With each case, the main topics covered are listed (approximately in order of their significance in the case), with a maximum of three topic descriptors. In some cases, more than three topics are covered in a case and, in these situations, the three main topics are indicated.

Section A: Cases in Management Accounting

No.	Case name	Main topics	Author(s)	Page
1	Malvern Limited	Budgeting; decision making	Ciaran Connolly, Queen's University Belfast	3
2	Quoile Industries	Budgeting and standard costing; decision making	Noel Hyndman, Queen's University Belfast	9
3	Toffer Group plc	Absorption and marginal costing; budgeting; decision making	Ciaran Connolly, Queen's University Belfast	15
4	Castlegrove Enterprises	Absorption and variable costing income statements; decision making	Tom Kennedy, University of Limerick	23
5	Spektrik plc	Target costing	Falconer Mitchell, University of Edinburgh	31
6	The Castleward Cycle Company	Transfer pricing; variance analysis; decision making	Noel Hyndman, Queen's University Belfast	35
7	Drumview Limited	Variance analysis; budgeting	Ciaran Connolly, Queen's University Belfast	41
8	Elveron Limited	Divisional performance; variance analysis; budgeting	Barbara Flood and Bernard Pierce, Dublin City University	47
9	Autoparts SA	Divisional performance; compensation schemes	Tony O'Dea and Tony Brabazon, University College Dublin	55
10	IXL Limited	Return on investment; investment appraisal; decision making	Joan Ballantine, Queen's University Belfast	59
11	Lennon Department Stores Limited	Budgeting; decision making; risk and uncertainty	Bernard Pierce and Barbara Flood, Dublin City University	65

No.	Case name	Main topics	Author(s)	Page
12	Top Flite plc	Return on investment and residual income; balanced scorecard	Joan Ballantine, Queen's University Belfast	73
13	Mississippi Inc.	Breakeven analysis; decision making; balanced scorecard	Tony O'Dea and Tony Brabazon, University College Dublin	77
14	EasyONline	Breakeven analysis; sensitivity analysis; optimal pricing strategies	Tony O'Dea and Tony Brabazon, University College Dublin	81
15	Beara Bay Cheese	Breakeven analysis; decision making; activity-based costing	Margaret Healy, University College Cork	85
16	Newtown Manufacturing Limited	Activity-based costing; decision making	Tom Kennedy, University of Limerick	93
17	Smith Specialist Car Components	Activity-based costing; target costing and decision making; investment appraisal	Noel Hyndman, Queen's University Belfast	101
18	Halvey's Bakery	Decision making; activity-based costing	John Doran and Margaret Healy, University College Cork	109
19	Chicken Pieces	Cost allocation; breakeven analysis; decision making	Peter Clarke, University College Dublin	113

Section B: Cases in Business Finance

No.	Case name	Main topics	Author(s)	Page
20	The Pottery Company 1	Working capital management; financial evaluation of strategy	Ann-Marie Ward, Queen's University Belfast	121
21	The Pottery Company 2	Cash and profit budgets; working capital management	Ann-Marie Ward, Queen's University Belfast	129
22	Waterlife	Cost of capital; capital structure; financing decisions	Evarist Stoja, Queen's University Belfast	135
23	Margin Limited	Investment appraisal and cost of capital; company valuation; foreign exchange risk management	Derry Cotter, University College Cork	141

24	DalCais Aer plc	Cost of capital; capital structure; dividend policy	Antoinette Flynn and Mairead Tracey, University of Limerick	147
25	Bradaun	Investment appraisal; sensitivity analysis; corporate governance	Ray Donnelly, University College Cork	153
26	Blackwater Hotel Group	Investment appraisal and cost of capital; sensitivity analysis	Peter Green, University of Ulster at Jordanstown	159
27	Tanaam	Investment appraisal; financing decisions; diversification	Louis Murray, University College Dublin	161
28	Calvin plc	Investment appraisal; capital structure; dividend policy	Peter Green, University of Ulster at Jordanstown	169
29	Xia Limited	Investment appraisal; foreign exchange risk	John Cotter, University College Dublin	173
30	Young & Co.	Investment appraisal; company valuation; dividend policy	Maeve McCutcheon, University College Cork	179
31	Good-to-Go	Financing decisions; capital structure; business strategy	Maeve McCutcheon, University College Cork	185
32	Plastic Products	Investment appraisal and cost of capital; company valuation; dividend policy	Derry Cotter, University College Cork	191
33	Homemade Pies plc	Valuation of pension funds; defined contribution and defined benefit pension schemes	John Cotter, University College Dublin	197
34	Mega Meals Limited	Risk management; interest rate swaps; foreign currency swaps	Paul McDonnell and Donal McKillop, Queen's University Belfast	203
35	Genero plc	Option pricing and sensitivities; Black-Scholes model; binomial trees	Paul McDonnell and Donal McKillop, Queen's University Belfast	207

About the Editors

Noel Hyndman is Professor of Management Accounting at Queen's University Belfast, having previously taught at the University of Ottawa in Canada and the University of Ulster. A Fellow of the Chartered Institute of Managements, he was awarded a PhD by Queen's University for his research in accounting and not-for-profit organisations. He has published widely in the areas of management accounting and not-for-profit accounting. Noel has had close association with the Institute of Chartered Accountants in Ireland (ICAI) in a range of activities for over twenty years, and has been involved in the Final Admitting Programme (FAE) programme of the ICAI since the mid 1980s in the areas of management accounting and business strategy.

Donal McKillop is Professor of Financial Services at Queen's University Belfast, having previously taught at the University of Ulster, and holds both undergraduate and postgraduate qualifications from the University of Ulster at Coleraine. His teaching specialism is derivative markets and instruments, and he has an extensive publication record, particularly in the area of credit unions. Among his books are: The Strategic Development of UK Credit Unions (Wiley, 1997, with Charles Ferguson) and The Structure, Performance and Governance of Irish Credit Unions (ICAI, 2006, with Peter Goth and Noel Hyndman). Donal was involved in the FAE programme for almost ten years in Belfast, where he both taught and co-ordinated the teaching of business finance.

Acknowledgements

The idea of the book was conceived in discussions at Queen's University Belfast between Noel Hyndman, Professor of Management Accounting, and Donal McKillop, Professor of Financial Services, and developed in talks with the ICAI, where Noel and Donal met with Ronan O'Loughlin (Director of Education and Training) and Kieran Lyons (Director of Publishing). Their valuable insights were much appreciated and are reflected in the final text. In addition, some initial and very welcome funding for the project was provided by the Irish Accountancy Educational Trust.

Introduction

The Increasing Use of Case Studies

At a university level, cases have become an invaluable resource to extend and improve a student's learning experience; and increasingly they have been used in advanced level courses in accounting, finance and business management once the basics of a subject have been explored. In addition, in professional accountancy programmes, case studies have similarly been used in capstone courses which students undertake near the completion of the professional programme. These courses build on skills and knowledge acquired in earlier studies and emphasise 'real world' situations. In addition, they often provide an opportunity for students to demonstrate competencies and communication skills.

However, the availability of 'good' new cases in both management accounting and business finance that are appropriate to a UK and Irish environment is limited. Many North American cases, while having great merit, are presented using scenarios and styles that are often not the most useful in a UK and Irish academic and professional examination setting. Other excellent cases that are widely used have become 'dated.' This book attempts to fill this gap.

There are two main reasons why case studies are a valuable means of practice. Firstly, knowledge grows and is better remembered when it is worked over and applied. Traditional textbooks are a necessary aid in the delivery of a course, but case studies are valuable in the application of the information presented. Secondly, a case study can help garner the whole picture for the student. While worked examples at the end of a chapter may develop an understanding of a particular topic, case studies go further to incorporate many issues in one integrated scenario.

The Aim of the Book

Cases in Management Accounting and Business Finance offers a range of case study material specific to the core areas of management accounting and business finance. It is targeted at postgraduate and final year undergraduate accounting and business students, as well those preparing for case examinations and assessments of the professional accountancy bodies. The unique text, which particularly reflects the development of the ICAI syllabus at the final examination levels, contains contributions from leading accounting and finance academics in Ireland and the UK (many of whom have contributed cases that were developed for use in university programmes). It is with considerable thanks that so many leading academics, with very busy schedules, agreed to contribute to this text. The book is broad in scope and considers areas as diverse as budgeting, divisionalisation and transfer pricing, cost allocation, risk management, takeovers, mergers, share valuations and interest rate swaps. The hope is that the use of this text will support an enriched contextual study of both management accounting and business finance.

Aspects of the book

Principles followed in the preparation of the book are:

- Largely, cases are specific to either management accounting or business finance, although a slight degree of overlap is contained in some of the cases (given the related and, at times, fuzzy dividing line between course material contained in management accounting and business finance courses, this is perhaps inevitable and desirable).
- The cases are prepared on the basis that students will have already studied at least one introductory course and one intermediate course in both management accounting and business finance.
- The cases are written so that they can be utilised in an 'open-book' environment if desired (that is, students will be able to consult their own material, including books and previously prepared notes, when answering).
- Many of the cases, although perhaps focusing on one main topic, contain a variety of management accounting or business finance topics.
- A variety of lengths of case are included, allowing a degree of flexibility of how they are used to support teaching and learning objectives.
- Many of the cases require an answer using report or memorandum format, thus helping students develop communication skills that will be particularly valuable in their career development.
- All cases require students to provide a mixture of quantitative and discursive answers.

Section A

Cases in Management Accounting

Case 1
Malvern Limited
Ciaran Connolly, Queen's University Belfast

Background

Malvern Limited, a Belfast-based manufacturing company, was established some 20 years ago by Bill Malvern, a talented and flamboyant engineer, with the proceeds of an attractive early retirement package. Bill worked tirelessly to grow the business and, until his retirement in 2XX0, the company manufactured a range of high quality products, all of which had been designed by Bill. In the last 10 years, Bill groomed his only son, Philip, to take over the business and when he did succeed his father in 2XX0, Philip did not have the same enthusiasm as his father and never settled into the role. Consequently, much to the disappointment of Bill, Philip decided to leave the company late in 2XX2. Bill, who was the chairman and major shareholder in Malvern Limited at that time, immediately appointed Robert Malvern, his grandson, to run the company. Robert had always been very close to his grandfather and, despite his young age and impetuous nature, had been involved in a number of successful business ventures prior to joining Malvern Limited, some of which had been partially funded by Bill.

Over the next two years, Robert significantly rationalised the activities of the company, reducing the workforce and eliminating all but one of Malvern Limited's products. Robert purchased Malvern Limited from his grandfather at the end of 2XX4, but he soon became restless and, in order to fund other new business ventures, decided to sell the company to Kate Black. It is now the beginning of May 2XX6 and Robert and Kate have agreed a date of sale of 31st May 2XX6, subject to Kate satisfactorily completing her review of the business.

The Product

Malvern Limited now manufactures a single product for the European haulage industry, a quick release towing mechanism that has proved very popular with British and Irish hauliers because it aids towing stability and enables easy coupling and de-coupling of loaded trailers. The towing mechanism, which was initially developed by Bill Malvern, has to be manufactured to stringent quality and safety standards.

The Company's Resources

Malvern Limited is situated on the outskirts of Belfast, with easy access to the main arterial roads in and out of the city. The company owns land, part of which contains the factory and administrative offices and part of which is currently undeveloped. The land was purchased some 15 years ago and is potentially worth much more that its current balance sheet value, depending upon whether approval could be obtained for commercial or residential redevelopment. The factory and administrative offices are large and in a reasonable state of repair, and there is scope to expand production within the existing factory building if necessary.

However, unfortunately, the machinery used in the manufacture of the towing mechanism is old and in need of immediate replacement, at a cost of approximately €130,000. The old machinery could be retained as back up, since it has no resale value and there is sufficient space to store it.

Apart from Robert, Malvern Limited currently employs four permanent staff, hiring temporary and short term contract labour when required. Fred, the factory supervisor, has been with the company since he left school and is due to retire in two years' time. He dislikes change and can be difficult to work with. Two of the other four permanent employees are Gary, a young enthusiastic operative who joined the company two years ago, and Tony, the accounts assistant who joined six months ago.

The Company's Systems

Tony is a bright, resourceful employee and, since joining Malvern Limited, has begun to develop the company's budgeting and reporting systems. Traditionally, little importance has been placed upon the preparation of budgets, management accounts or reports. This largely stems from the hands-on role adopted by Bill when he was involved with the company. Phillip had little interest in developing the company's systems, while Robert is inclined to take the view that if he can see the men working diligently in the factory, then business must be fine. At present, production levels tend to be kept at a constant rate regardless of demand and purchases of raw materials are made on an ad hoc basis. It is mainly by good luck rather than good management that sufficient raw materials are available, although it has become accepted practice to carry high stocks of raw materials and towing mechanisms as there is adequate storage space in the factory.

The Competitive Environment

Malvern Limited is one of only a few British and Irish companies which manufacture the towing mechanism. While there are only three manufacturers of the type of vehicle that uses the company's towing mechanism, these vehicles are purchased by a large number of hauliers throughout Europe. Following a short period of sluggish sales, sales of the towing mechanism have been fairly constant over the last two years.

Future Prospects

Kate is optimistic about the company's prospects, believing that, if the company can keep pace with changes in the industry, demand for the towing mechanism will increase considerably in the medium to long term. Furthermore, having examined the financial information prepared by Tony, Kate is confident that the draft balance sheet as at 31st May 2XX6 is a reasonable assessment of the company's assets and liabilities on this date (see Appendix 1). She has negotiated a €30,000 overdraft facility to be available to the company from 1st June 2XX6, the date from which she takes over as owner. However, the bank has stated that any further borrowing by Malvern Limited will have to be supported by appropriate detailed budgeted information.

Kate has considerable accounting experience and, with Tony, has gathered the following data from Robert and the company's records to enable budgets to be prepared for the four month period to 30th September 2XX6:

Estimated Production Data

Selling price per towing mechanism	€300
Materials usage per towing mechanism	1 1/2 kgs
Cost of materials per kg	€40
Production wages and variable overheads per towing mechanism	€70
Fixed overheads per month	€3,500

	June	July	August	September
Sales of towing mechanisms	120	125	115	100
Production of towing mechanisms	110	130	116	90
Purchases of raw materials (kgs)	150	160	150	140

Credit Terms

All sales are on credit and two months' credit is allowed. All purchases of raw materials are on credit and are paid for one month following purchase. Wages, variable and fixed overheads are paid in the month in which they are incurred.

Purchase of New Machinery

Subject to the sale of the company being agreed, Kate has purchased new machinery at a cost of €130,000, with delivery and installation in June 2XX6 and payment in the following month. On 1st July 2XX6, the company will issue 10% debentures to the value of €150,000, with the €150,000 being credited to the company's bank account on the same date. Debenture interest is paid annually in arrears, with repayment due in June 2X11.

Depreciation June to September 2XX6

Buildings	€500
Machinery (including depreciation on new machinery)	€16,000
Vehicles	€5,500

Required

Question 1

(a) Prepare the raw materials budget and the finished goods budget for each of the four months from June to September 2XX6 inclusive. Each budget should be expressed in either kilograms or towing mechanisms, as appropriate.

(10 marks)

(b) Prepare the sales revenue budget and production cost budget for each of the four months from June to September 2XX6 inclusive, and calculate the budgeted closing stock, debtors and creditors as at 30th September 2XX6.

(10 marks)

(b) Prepare the cash budget for each of the four months from June to September 2XX6 inclusive.

(10 marks)

Question 2

Kate wishes to use the budget information for monitoring and controlling purposes. Write a memorandum to Tony explaining how Kate might use:

(a) The budget to monitor and control the company's activities (it should also identify the tasks which Kate might require Tony to undertake in implementing the process);

(10 marks)

(b) A responsibility accounting approach (it should also highlight some of the problems that she might encounter in doing so).

(10 marks)

Question 3

Kate now believes that the company will have 30% spare capacity from August to October 2XX6 inclusive. For an additional investment of €30,000, she can modify the new machinery, making it more flexible and thus enabling the company to manufacture towing mechanisms that would be suitable for a wider range of vehicles.

Identify the types of information that Kate would need to consider in making a decision to purchase the additional machinery and the likely sources of such information.

(20 marks)

Question 4

Prepare a budgeted profit and loss account for the four months to 30th September 2XX6 (one for the four month period) and a budgeted balance sheet as at 30th September 2XX6. Ignore taxation.

(30 marks)

Total 100 marks

Appendix 1
Budgeted Balance Sheet of Malvern Limited as at 31st May 2XX6

	€ Cost	€ Accumulated Depreciation	€ Net Book Value
Fixed Assets			
Land and buildings	120,000	(20,000)	100,000
Machinery	50,000	(44,000)	6,000
Vehicles	52,000	(16,000)	36,000
	222,000	(80,000)	142,000
Current Assets			
Stock of raw materials (100 kgs)	4,000		
Stock of finished goods (110 towing mechanisms)	12,100		
Trade debtors (April €5,900 and May €13,100)	19,000		
	35,100		
Creditors: amounts falling due within 1 year			
Trade creditors for raw materials	(3,400)		
Bank overdraft	(17,250)		14,450
			156,450
Capital and Reserves			
€1 ordinary shares			100,000
Retained earnings			56,450
			156,450

Note: finished goods stocks are valued at marginal cost for budget purposes.

Case 2

Quoile Industries

Noel Hyndman, Queen's University Belfast

The Company

You (Sonia O'Hare) have recently been appointed finance director of Quoile Industries, Ireland's oldest privately owned, family-operated trailer manufacturer. The company was founded 20 years ago by the eccentric, yet brilliant, Crawford Bell, who still maintains a controlling interest, sits on the board of directors as chairman, and was responsible for your appointment. However, nowadays Crawford only fulfils a part-time role and spends some considerable time away from the company on his various outside interests (which include motor cycling on his 1,000 cc Harley Davidson, playing hockey as a demon forward in the fifths at Downpatrick Hockey Club, and working in the Ukraine helping to build houses for disadvantaged communities with Habitat for Humanity).

As for the company he established, Quoile Industries designs and manufactures dry freight vans, flatbeds, refrigerated vans and curtain-sided trailers. It is the largest producer of refrigerated vans, and the third-largest trailer manufacturer, in Ireland. This position is a result of management's focus on providing innovative solutions to customer problems. It has invested heavily in research and development to ensure that its products are at the leading edge of available technology.

Budgeting and Standard Costing System

Quoile Industries operates linked standard costing and budgetary control systems. Management accounts, which are reviewed at monthly board meetings, are produced from the system, and these analyse variances by cost type for each major product. The budgeting cycle begins two months before the commencement of the financial year and the completed budget is normally submitted to the board of directors by the third week in December, when some final 'tweaking' may occur. Traditionally, the budget has been developed by three key members of staff (the finance director, sales director and production director). A number of meetings between the three directors are arranged for November and December where varying scenarios are developed and budget iterations made. The key information for budget preparation has tended to be the sales budget, and once sales figures for each product line are agreed, the production director and finance director take responsibility for the completion of the other budgets.

Establishing an appropriate sales budget has been problematical in the past. Budgeted volumes for products and budgeted sales prices have been difficult to establish with any degree of accuracy. The market for many of the company's products has been quite competitive, with imported trailers from China being increasingly available at very keen prices (although quality and service with respect to these is often much lower than that with Quoile's products). In addition, establishing an appropriate product and price focus in the budgeting process has been difficult given the absence of any systematic strategic planning procedures within the company. Rolling strategic planning was discontinued several years ago because the external environment was so difficult to predict, particularly in the areas of emerging technology, health and safety issues, and competitive pressures. Since then it has been left to the sales director to come up with sales estimates and target prices at budgeting time. This he does through personal judgement, particularly relying on previous sales trends over the last few years to influence such judgement. Sales details for the previous year relating to one of Quoile's newest products (the FB2008) are provided in Appendix 1. The FB2008 is a high strength, low weight flatbed trailer. It has: a 3,000 kgs working load limit; an aluminum front rail; 100% plug-in connectors; durable outrigger attachments; an integral cinch track; front stainless steel corners; floor attachment plates; and a durable suspension design. It competes in a fairly well-defined market segment.

Sales budgets provide an important target for sales staff, with the achievement of these being linked to annual bonus payments. The sales budget is profiled on a monthly basis and broken down by product and by sales representative. While detailed information is produced each month comparing actual sales against budget (by product and by sales representative), annual bonuses are awarded to the entire sales team (including the sales director) on the basis of total annual sales against total annual sales budget at the end of the year. The argument for using a team-based bonus is that the sales team should be rewarded collectively for their effort and this approach encourages team spirit and co-operative effort. It is interesting to note that over the last few years when sales have increased quite significantly (and the size of the market for trailers has been buoyant), the increase in the sales budget has been quite modest. Sales budgets have been viewed throughout the company as being quite 'soft', although the sales director argues that this provides an essential ingredient to increase motivation and points to the sales growth as evidence of this. He further suggests that the sales team is doing well in terms of market share, and highlights the sales performance relating to FB2008 as proof. The net result of this is that substantial bonuses have been achieved by the sales team.

Once the sales budget has been finalised, production, selling and administration budgets are prepared. These are then introduced into the overall budgeting framework to produce a budgeted income statement, balance sheet and cash flow forecast. Over the last number of years, this has produced a satisfactory level of budgeted net profit and positive cash flow and although variances arise, the company has enjoyed acceptable profits and a comfortable cash position. However it is thought that, given recent upward pressure on international interest rates, it is likely that such halcyon days may soon be a thing of the past and belt tightening may be required. Generally, budgets for non-production overheads have not received much attention in the budgeting process, largely being increased in line with the sales budget. However, given anticipated future pressures, it is proposed that in the incoming year budgets for advertising and training be reduced by 15%, while investment in research and development be reduced by 25%.

Many of the production costs used in budget preparation flow from the standard costing system which was established some years ago. Features of the system include:

- Quantities of material and labour for all products were set three years ago and although design and production processes have been modified slightly, the unit quantities have not been changed.
- Prices for the materials and rates for labour were set at the same time (three years ago) and have been increased each year in line with the retail price index.
- Variances are reported in the management accounting package that is used to report to board members within a few days of the month end, with the cost centre managers receiving the information several days later. In reality, few cost centre managers pay particular attention to variances, although some of the figures are quite substantial.

Possible Expansion

The production director is keen to expand the company's product range and has been encouraging the strategic acquisition of a forklift truck manufacturer to augment its product offering. Many of Quoile's existing customers use forklift trucks in their businesses. Having researched the types of forklift used by its existing customers, the production director believes that a relatively small, light, electric forklift with a narrow chassis would be particularly attractive (given that with many of its customers, space is at a premium and forklift trucks are not used continuously throughout the working day).

Quoile has identified two possible acquisition candidates (both in North America): Boucher Forklifts (based in Ottawa in Canada); and Jackson Engineering (based in Tallahassee in the USA). These companies are both relatively young and have invested heavily in new technology in the exact area of forklift truck manufacturing in which Quoile is interested (although, to date, neither company has been profitable). In terms of market, to date both companies have targeted North America as their sole sales focus. Boucher Forklifts produce the Carleton forklift which sells at C$14,000. Jackson Engineering produces the Wakulla forklift, a slightly lighter truck, with fewer standard features. It sells for US$11,250. The current exchange rates for the Canadian and US dollars are: €1 = C$1.4; and €1 = US$1.25.

While, at present, Quoile does not sell forklift trucks to its existing customers, the production director believes that such a product would complement its existing sales and, in the not too distant future, enhance profitability with the current customer base.

Other information relating to the possible acquisitions is as follows:

- Budgeted production, selling and administration costs associated with the Carleton (Boucher Forklifts) and the Wakulla (Jackson Engineering) for next year are presented in Appendix 2. These figures have been prepared by a team from Quoile after discussions with the acquisition targets. In addition, they take into account efficiency savings from further investment by Quoile in new technology of C$20 million (Boucher Forklifts – Carleton) and US$25 million (Jackson Engineering – Wakulla) that is deemed necessary and would be invested immediately should either company be acquired.
- Budgeted sales volumes for next year are presented in Appendix 3. Estimating sales volumes is problematical for each of the products, particularly given the relative youth of both acquisition targets and their underdeveloped customer base. As a consequence, the management of each company has, after discussions with Quoile, estimated a range of possible sales volumes and their associated probabilities. Jackson Engineering is located near a number of potential customers in Florida and has already secured some orders for next year, and is fairly confident of others. The situation regarding Boucher Forklifts is less certain.
- At present, negotiations regarding acquisition are at a fairly advanced stage and Quoile's team believes that Boucher Forklifts could be acquired for about C$140 million, whereas Jackson Engineering would cost US$80 million.
- It is likely that, should either company be acquired, the management team would remain for some time.

Request for Your Views

As the most recent senior appointment to Quoile Industries, and therefore a person who would be well placed to provide a bit of objectivity, Crawford Bell, the chairman and founder, is keen to have your views on what should be done in the company. Although somewhat detached from day-to-day management issues, he still wants the company to make decisions that will result in a healthy and prosperous future for the company and its employees. In appointing you to the position of financial director, he saw someone with business acumen and integrity that reflected his views on what a company should be about. Now, with the sun setting on the beautiful Zbruch River, Crawford laid his last brick for the day in the wall of a new house in Volochisk, Ukraine, and glanced across the water to Podvolochisk in the distance as he prepared to turn in for the night. He went to his bed content, knowing that at home you would be looking after the best interests of Quoile Industries, and he looked forward to his return from the Ukraine in two weeks' time and an analysis from you on what direction the company should take.

Required

As Sonia O'Hare (the financial director of Quoile Industries), draft an internal memorandum to Crawford Bell dealing with the following issues:

1. With respect to the budgeting and standard costing system (including the bonus system for sales staff), identify any possible weaknesses of the current system, explain the possible consequences of these weaknesses and make recommendations for improvement. Given that Crawford Bell likes focus and detests information overload, he asks that a maximum of eight major weaknesses be identified and the weaknesses, consequences and recommendations be presented succinctly in tabular format.

    (40 marks)

2. Specifically with respect to the FB2008 flatbed trailer:

    (a) Calculate the market size and market share variances on the basis of the information provided in Appendix 1.

    (10 marks)

    (b) Comment on the relevance of theses variances, particularly in the light of the sales director's claims that the sales team is doing well in terms of market share.

    (6 marks)

3. With respect to the possible acquisition of a forklift truck manufacturer:

    (a) Calculate the expected profitability of both the Boucher and the Jackson proposals, indicating also the range of possible profit outcomes, and comment on these figures.

    (14 marks)

    (b) Calculate return on investment and payback for the two options, clearly stating any assumptions that you make. Comment briefly on theses figures.

    (6 marks)

    (c) Calculate the breakeven sales volume and sales value figures for Boucher and Jackson. Comment briefly on these calculations.

    (6 Marks)

    (d) Based on the available information, suggest which, or whether either, of the proposals is attractive to Quoile Industries. The evaluation should draw on the above calculations, together with any relevant qualitative and strategic issues.

    (18 marks)

    Total 100 marks

Appendix 1
Summary Sales Variance Information Relating to Product FB2008 for Previous Year

Sales Price Variance (at €500 per unit)	€2,500,000 (F)
Sales Volume Variance (standard margin €3,000 per unit)	€1,500,000 (F)

When setting the budget for the FB2008 Quoile believed the market for flatbed trailers to be 45,000. However, it transpired that the actual sales were 8% of the actual market. The actual sales price paid by customers was €500 per trailer above the budgeted sales price per unit.

Appendix 2
Budgeted Production, Selling and Administration Costs for Next Year

	Boucher Forklifts Carleton C$	Jackson Engineering Wakulla US$
Variable costs (per unit):		
Production	8,500	7,000
Selling	1,260	625
Fixed costs (total):	C$ (million)	US$ (million)
Production	27.8	25.8
Selling	7.2	3
Administration	10.4	7.1

Appendix 3
Budgeted Sales Volumes for Next Year

Boucher Forklifts – Carleton		Jackson Engineering – Wakulla	
Sales volume	Probability	Sales volume	Probability
10,000	0.05	10,000	0.05
12,000	0.15	12,000	0.10
14,000	0.20	14,000	0.40
16,000	0.25	16,000	0.40
18,000	0.35	18,000	0.05

Case 3
Toffer Group plc
Ciaran Connolly, Queen's University Belfast

James Grant FCA is the chief executive of Toffer Group plc (Toffer), a large Irish company that manufactures satellite dishes, and he has recently appointed Ian Legg as personnel director of the company. Prior to joining Toffer, Ian had spent the previous six years as the personnel manager for a reputable medium-sized company, KTE Limited (KTE), and was under no illusions about the pressures and expectations that came with the new post.

Wherever he had worked, Ian had always tried to avoid the company accountants, as those he met tended to be reserved and uncommunicative. His involvement with the accountants at KTE was limited to polite enquiries on payroll and employment records, and the occasional commandeering of his office to 'house' the auditors. At Toffer, the accountants have a central role in the decision-making process. Before James Grant authorised any proposal, budgets were prepared, products were priced and ratios calculated, with considerable emphasis placed upon 'contribution.' It was contribution, not profit, which marked the difference between the acceptance and rejection of a proposal. Ian would have continued to leave the decision making to the accountants and bowed to their financial wisdom if it had not been for one particular event that occurred approximately fourteen months before he left KTE.

KTE was an established family business whose chairman, Sir Ryan O'Leary, was the last in the family line going back over a number of generations. As retirement age approached, Sir Ryan merged his firm with Toffer approximately three years ago, building in as many safeguards for his family and employees as possible. Consequently, the extension of Toffer's influence over KTE had been slow and gradual. James Grant was aware of the potential of KTE Limited, particularly if their production methods were modernised, but was reluctant to make radical changes too quickly preferring to allow retirements to take their natural course. Indeed, James Grant had shown remarkable and uncharacteristic restraint in waiting to make the changes, but it could not last forever.

The end came in a deceptively mild way. The original budget, which is shown in Appendix 1, for KTE had already been approved for the forthcoming period.

Unexpectedly, the routine board meeting for November was presented with market research findings conducted by a firm appointed by James Grant, who expanded on the research figures:

'The conclusions from the market research are that next year the maximum number of units that could be sold by KTE is:

Alpha: 5,000 units
Beta: 4,000 units
Gamma: 4,000 units

However, as you can see, these figures are different to the proposed production figures in the approved budget. The accountants suggest we have no alternative but to reschedule production to maximise contribution based on the best way sales demand can be satisfied. Any threat to customer satisfaction can temporarily be solved by another of our UK plants.'

James Grant continued:

'Unfortunately the labour supply in Department Y is fixed and because of the way KTE has been organised, it takes a long period of training to achieve the skill required. Indeed, management have exacerbated the problem by voluntarily agreeing with the trade unions upon restrictions in the labour supply. We therefore cannot change the Department Y constraint and consequently Departments X and Z may be adversely affected.'

It was an uncharacteristically mild intervention by James Grant, and few fully anticipated the implications. However, six months later Ian most certainly did. Redundancies, strikes and industrial strife had destroyed a morale and esprit de corps at KTE that had taken many years to build. Abandoning caution Ian decided to unreservedly let James Grant know his views on the matter, the essence of which was that a company's profits are directly related to the way it treats the workforce, and that people must be treated as individuals and invested with some measure of dignity to obtain their best.

James Grant made no attempt to conceal his look of astonishment, but continued to listen with a mixture of indifference and tolerance. His only reply was that the short term profit improvement would help people accept the change and that perhaps his accountants could improve their 'people skills.' James Grant left abruptly, leaving Ian contemplating his future. Surprisingly, just over a year later, he was the new personnel director of Toffer, again acting as the buffer between profits and people.

Ian's role in Toffer was varied and interesting; a major part being concerned with the identification, take-over and integration of suitable businesses to enhance Toffer's expansion plans. One such business was Bebe Limited (Bebe), a company with a chequered history that in recent years had made a name for itself by concentrating on one product, the Net, and backing it with substantial advertising. James Grant was rather taken with the quality, versatility and reliability of this new product, believing it would round off Toffer's communications activities. However, he was well aware that Bebe would need more finance if the company was to expand.

The directors of Bebe soon became involved in talks with Toffer, making the company's financial records freely available for review. While Ian's responsibilities were to investigate the manpower side of Bebe, including the age profile of the directors and executives, service contracts, training facilities and manpower policies, since his outburst at KTE, he had tried to develop a wider brief. The accounting team moved fast and investigated every possible figure. Their approach was now predictable, focusing on contribution margins and formatting income statements on a marginal costing basis.

Appendix 2 shows the standard cost card for the Net and Appendix 3 a financial profit statement for the previous year.

At a meeting to discuss the possible acquisition of Bebe, James Grant pondered aloud:

'The problem is just how accurate are their budgets and forecasts because we know that Bebe's budgetary planning and control systems are virtually non-existent. If we can believe them, this year's sales will match their production capacity of about 12,000 Nets and next year's demand will be even greater, so that they will have to rely on stocks. If so, this is the time to buy them on a price earnings basis.'

There was silence during which various projections prepared by the finance director were studied. James Grant then continued: 'My hunch is that a new alternative product just introduced to the market by a competitor is going to make inroads into the sales of Bebe. If so, the company may only match last year's figures, which would mean that a cash flow crisis in a year's time would make Bebe ripe for the picking.'

Ian soon lost the thread of the argument. With some apprehension he asked how it could be that there were two results for the previous year and why, if the published accounts were open to doubt, they were accepted by the auditors. All the accountants at the meeting laughed pleasantly and genuinely. 'Let's say', said James Grant, 'that for decision making only the marginal or direct cost approach is valid and the IAS 2 [SSAP 9] hang-up, where profits are anticipated, can lead companies into all sorts of difficulties.' James Grant's glance dismissed any further questions and Ian felt it wise to nod in agreement although not understanding for one moment what it all meant.

Within six weeks of taking over Bebe, and after offering many assurances, James Grant was talking of closing departments, transferring work to other divisions, cost-reduction schemes and reviewing manpower levels. Naturally morale was falling rapidly. It finally came to a head over the Navigator component. James Grant was considering buying-in this sub-assembly from another group company, Turpin Limited, and closing a department within Bebe. Ian was quite prepared to risk all on opposing what he felt were blatantly unethical business tactics.

At the next management meeting, Ian decided to state his case:

'It has been an open secret that James and I have not seen eye to eye in business decisions that affect personnel and labour relations. I am obliged to say that I am opposed to redundancies in this department. This department has a creditable record and is staffed by young, enthusiastic employees who were given firm assurances upon the take-over that work would not be transferred elsewhere. There is more to running a successful business than crude money-grabbing.'

Ian's tone was respectful but by no means humble, and the obvious sincerity of his feelings silenced all present at the meeting as they awaited James Grant's response. James Grant looked at Ian for a moment as though debating with himself just how to handle a man with such an unswerving belief in his cause. Finally he said:

> 'Perhaps you are right, there are issues here that are more complex than might appear at first sight. Let us re-examine all the figures and see if there is room for compromise.'

It was an unexpectedly mild reply but Ian had not missed the exchange of looks between James Grant and his accountants. It would be no surprise if there was now a temporary reprieve based on some sound financial judgement. But what long-term future remained for both Ian and the department?

Relevant extracts of the report on the Navigator component are presented in Appendix 4.

Required

Question 1
Why might the accountants at Toffer concentrate on contribution and marginal costing as the basis of their decision making?

(4 marks)

Question 2
Why would the accountants prefer marginal costing to absorption costing?

(4 marks)

Question 3
By what means might the accountants analyse costs into their fixed and variable components for the purpose of identifying contribution?

(4 marks)

Question 4
From Appendix 1, calculate the contribution per hour of the Department Y constraint.

(4 marks)

Question 5
Prepare a new budget for KTE based on the most profitable way sales demand can be satisfied, and calculate the extra profit this would yield.

(8 marks)

Question 6
Assuming that each employee of KTE contributes 1,920 hours of work per annum, how many redundancies in Departments X and Z could arise if the new budget was strictly adhered to?

(4 marks)

Question 7
Using Appendix 2 and Appendix 3, prepare a profit statement for Bebe under marginal costing principles.

(4 marks)

Question 8
Assuming this year's sales of Nets match the production capacity of 12,000 units:

(a) Prepare a financial statement using absorption costing principles;
(b) Prepare a financial statement using marginal costing principles.

(10 marks)

Question 9
Assuming that demand for Nets next year did increase so that both production of 12,000 and stocks of 4,000 Nets were sold:

(a) Prepare a financial statement using absorption costing principles;
(b) Prepare a financial statement using marginal costing principles.

(10 marks)

Question 10
From the answers you have prepared for questions 7, 8 and 9, complete the table below and comment on the information supplied.

	Absorption €'000s	Marginal €'000s
Last year	880	
This year		
Next year		
Total over three years		

(8 marks)

Question 11
Prepare arguments to support marginal costing and arguments to support absorption costing for routine profit reporting purposes.

(6 marks)

Question 12

Explain how Toffer might introduce a new budgetary planning and control system in Bebe, and outline the behavioural problems that might be encountered when doing so.

(16 marks)

Question 13

If production of Navigator ceases, the machinery would be rendered redundant and consequently a loss on sale of approximately €25,000 would be incurred. Surely this is extra support for the argument for retaining manufacture at Bebe?

(4 marks)

Question 14

From a financial standpoint, should the Navigator component be manufactured at Bebe or Turpin Limited?

(10 marks)

Question 15

What other factors, financial or otherwise, would you consider relevant to the decision?

(4 marks)

Total 100 marks

Appendix 1
KTE's Original Budget

	Alpha € unit	Beta € unit	Gamma € unit
Selling price	620	620	940
Direct materials	99	252	162
Direct labour:			
• Department X	(30 hrs x €9) 270	(15 hrs x €9) 135	(32 hrs x €9) 288
• Department Y	(6 hrs x €12) 72	(8 hrs x €12) 96	(10 hrs x €12) 120
• Department Z	(15 hrs x €9) 135	(8 hrs x €9) 72	(32 hrs x €9) 288
Prime cost	576	555	858
Variable overhead	14	10	18
Marginal cost	590	565	876
Contribution/unit	30	55	64
Proposed production (units)	5,000	2,000	3,000
Total contribution/product	€150,000	€110,000	€192,000

	€
Total contribution	452,000
Fixed overhead	152,000
Budgeted profit	300,000

Appendix 2
Net Standard Cost Card

	€ unit
Selling price	1,000
Direct materials	300
Direct labour	100
Prime cost	400
Variable production overheads	100
Marginal cost	500
Fixed overhead:*	
production	240
selling & distribution	100
Total cost	840
Profit/unit	160

* Based on an output of 50 Nets per day for a 48-week working year. Over the anticipated range of sales, selling costs, etc., these costs are, for all meaningful purposes, fixed.

Appendix 3
Bebe Financial Profit Statement
(amended from previous year's accounts)

	No. of units	€ per unit	€'000s
Sales	8,000	1,000	8,000
Production costs:	12,000		
Variable		500	6,000
Fixed		240	2,880
		740	8,880
less Closing stock	4,000	740	2,960
Cost of goods sold			5,920
Factory profit			2,080
Selling, distribution & administration costs			1,200
Net profit			880

Note: the published annual accounts report a profit of €867,500. The Toffer accountants have taken out various figures and approximated the remainder in line with the standard, with the result being much easier to interpret.

Appendix 4
Navigator Component Report (Extract)

1. The component is manufactured by machinery which cost €50,000 five years ago and is being depreciated over ten years on a straight-line basis. If production ceases there is little chance of the machinery being used elsewhere, and the resale value would be negligible.

2. Production of Navigator is currently running at 1,000 components per month. A study of the manufacture in the previous month revealed that the following costs were directly attributable to the manufacture of 1,000 components:

	€
Direct material	32,500
Direct labour	40,000
Indirect labour	10,000
Power	1,500
Maintenance	1,000
Sundries	500

3. The total costs for the same month of the department within which the Navigator is made were as follows:

	€
Direct labour	105,000
Indirect labour	35,000
Direct material	80,000
Electricity	30,000
Maintenance	7,000
Insurance of machinery	5,000
Depreciation of machinery	20,000
Canteen and welfare	3,500
Sundries	6,000
Apportioned fixed overhead	30,000

4. If the production of Navigator ceased, there would be the following savings:

Insurance	€75 per month
Electricity	€675 per month

    In addition there would be savings in canteen and welfare costs, which vary approximately with the numbers employed.

5. Turpin Limited has submitted a quotation of €85 per Navigator component. In addition, there would be shipping, transport and inspection costs in the region of €2.50 per component.

Case 4
Castlegrove Enterprises
Tom Kennedy, University of Limerick

Overview of the Company

Two partners, Larry Maloney and Sean McKenna, set up Castlegrove Enterprises some twenty years ago, shortly after they were made redundant from Digimac. Digimac had supplied parts to the Irish and European car industry and decided to consolidate all their European manufacturing operations in Eastern Europe. Maloney and McKenna had been employees of Digimac for 15 years and had been given a significant redundancy payment. Their families were well settled in the Galway area and were reluctant to move. Maloney, had a degree in manufacturing engineering, and after ten years of service with Digimac in a variety of positions was promoted to manufacturing manager. McKenna, who had a diploma in purchasing and logistics, had initially worked as a buyer before transferring to materials. He had been promoted to material manager some four years before being made redundant by Digimac.

Both were keen golfers and had often spoken about the need to get away from the continually increasing work pressures experienced in Digimac. They discussed the possibility of setting up their own business on a number of occasions, but did not have the capital or courage to make the transition. Now, that the opportunity presented itself and with the encouragement of their families and the local enterprise board, they took the initiative. In doing so, they decided that Maloney was to be the managing director, with specific responsibility for production, engineering and facilities. McKenna was to be deputy-managing director with responsibility for purchasing, materials and administration.

Business Performance/History

After an initially difficult first two years, Castlegrove became a thriving business, primarily through the manufacture and supply of a small range of customised products for the building industry. They had developed a very solid customer base and were the preferred supplier with a number of large building contractors. Ireland, labelled the 'Celtic Tiger,' had just entered a phase of sustained rapid economic development. This allowed Castlegrove to capitalise on the huge demand for building and related products. Given their high dependency on this market and the public debate as to its sustainability, Maloney and McKenna were determined to diversify when the right opportunity presented itself. They had built up a successful management team and re-organised their responsibilities in late 2XX1. Kevin Holmes was hired to take responsibility for production, having previously worked for a competitor in Dublin. Mary McGuire had become familiar with the business as audit manager for a number of years and was attracted by the offer to work nearer to home. She joined Castlegrove as accounting manager. Liam Jones was promoted to sales manager, based on his excellent record as the senior sales representative for the past five years with Castlegrove. A local retired bank manager and a solicitor, who was recommended by one of Maloney's golfing partners, joined the board. The senior management team met formally every second Monday morning and the board usually met every three months. Castlegrove continued to maintain its original policy of staying with and developing its core business.

However, the sudden death of the owner of a small local garden accessories business, Rosemount, led to their decision to take over that business in late 2XX2. Rosemount had traded successfully for about 20 years under the astute direction of Michael Murphy in premises adjacent to Castlegrove. Murphy's family had no involvement in the business and his management style did not facilitate a management buy out. Murphy had acted as mentor to Maloney and McKenna and they had valued his advice on a number of occasions. They were shocked by his sudden death and felt obligated to help his family. They moved quickly to take over the running of the business with the encouragement of his widow and completed the purchase some months later. They successfully integrated Rosemount into their own operations and it traded successfully for over two years.

All was to change with the entry of a new low cost multinational company, Zip, in late 2XX4. Zip set up its own manufacturing facility in a new industrial estate in the outskirts of Galway and it was to present very serious competitive problems for Rosemount. Zip had recognised the market potential nationally and was in the process of rolling out a targeted expansion programme. Rosemount could not match their range of products, aggressive marketing and special promotions. They lost over half their customers in the first half of 2XX5 and, despite extensive efforts to recover market share, faced the inevitable decision to close Rosemount. This decision was finally made by Castlegrove at a special board meeting in September 2XX5. However, it was decided to defer making the decision public until a proposal from the new product development team had been considered.

New Product Development

Maloney and McKenna were always conscious of the need to invest in research and development and had set up a small new product development team in 2XX3. This team was made up of two engineering graduates and a production management student. It was decided to strengthen that team with the addition of John Somers in 2XX5. John was an electronic engineering graduate and had worked with Maloney and McKenna in Digimac. He went to Australia to work in the printing business when he was made redundant. He returned to Ireland on the death of his mother in April 2XX5 and was impressed with the huge change in the economic landscape since his departure. He ran into Maloney at the local golf club and was taken by his offer to join them on a trial basis. His brief was to assess the feasibility of a number of product ideas that were at an advanced stage of development and to bring them to the board for consideration. When he assessed the situation, he decided that the laser multi-purpose ruler and sensor unit was the most advanced technically. Following feedback from a number of trade shows, and in conjunction with McGuire, he held a number of meetings with Jones and Holmes. This project team produced a comprehensive proposal for consideration at a specially convened board meeting in late October 2XX5. The proposal included draft operating income statements, market research, technical specifications, production and capital expenditure requirements. It made a strong recommendation to proceed with the manufacture of the laser unit. The board was impressed with the proposal and gave its approval. The unit was to be marketed under the name 'Pulse' and would be supplied to distributors in Ireland and England initially.

In making this strategic investment decision, the board was conscious of the need to find alternative work for the highly trained and long-serving production employees in Rosemount. The decision to develop 'Pulse' resulted in Castlegrove being able to retain them, based on the projections presented in the proposal and their suitability for the new production line. Critically, this meant that it did not have to pay out a significant lump sum redundancy payment or undertake a major re-training programme. Arising from the board decision in late October 2XX5, a capital expenditure programme was expedited. The commissioning of the automated equipment and the refurbishment of the production facility was to be completed in December 2XX5. Production and sales of 'Pulse' would commence in January 2XX6 and Rosemount would cease trading after Christmas 2XX5 in an orderly fashion.

Projected Operating Income of the 'Pulse' Product Line

The relevant costs and revenue associated with the 'Pulse' project are shown in Appendix 1. This shows that operating income in the year ended 2XX6 was anticipated to be €30,600 and €52,600 in the year ended 2XX7. Breakeven had been calculated at about 4,109 units and with sales estimated at 5,500 in 2XX6 and 6,500 in 2XX7, a very acceptable margin of safety was projected. This gave the project team and the board great confidence in the viability of the project. Somers was complimented by the board on his initiative and was asked to submit a timescale for the other new projects in the pipeline. He was offered and accepted the newly created position of product development manager and given an attractive remuneration package. His plans to return to Australia were put on hold for the foreseeable future.

During the preparation of the projected operating results, Jones spoke very strongly about the importance of setting realistic sales targets for the first year of any new product launch. He was very positive in regard to 2XX7 and, based on the market research data, was happy to commit to an approximate 18% projected increase for that year. He was less bullish about projections thereafter; noting that the 2XX7 projected performance was unlikely to be repeated. He thought it more reasonable to work on the basis of something in the order of a 15% annual increase for the foreseeable future. A lot of discussion took place before agreeing on a price of €85 per unit. Despite its uniqueness, some benchmarking was possible and this suggested a price in the range €90 to €100 per unit. The issue was unresolved until McGuire came up with a preliminary variable cost figure in the range €60 to €70 per unit. This information quickly led to an agreement to go with an aggressive pricing strategy, given that it met Castlegrove's policy of achieving a minimum profit-volume (or contribution to sales) ratio of 20% on all product lines.

During this process, Holmes became somewhat agitated when he learned of the level of sales anticipated by Jones in the earlier years of the project. His analysis of the new plant capability and the quality of the operatives being made available from Rosemount was that he could comfortably produce 10,000 units per annum. This estimate took into account planned downtime and an allowance for other eventualities. He argued that it was important to keep the highly skilled operatives at his disposal working effectively and efficiently. He was proud of his record, as production manager, in utilising the assets of the company to their full potential and did not wish to have his record tarnished. Jones was adamant that he could not commit to more sales and that most of them would be to order. He added that there would be some benefit in building up a small stock reserve in order to cater for any unexpected sales and to ensure continuity of supply. Holmes was somewhat pacified by this, and having reviewed his notes with his production supervisor, agreed to a production schedule of 7,000 units in 2XX6 and 8,500 units in 2XX7. His judgement was that this schedule would not necessitate any layoffs, but would involve running the machines at about 80% capacity. This, he accepted, was reasonable in the early stages of the life cycle of a new product.

The discussion became somewhat heated again when McGuire warned about the undesirable effect of building up too much inventory and the impact that could have on the reported profit. Even though she had raised this many times before, she had always failed to convince the largely production focussed management team to engage with her on the issue. She went on to talk about things like absorption costing and the need to understand the impact of using different levels of capacity for different applications. She advised the project team that Castlegrove always used the practical capacity level for financial reporting and stock valuation purposes. She emphasised that this was particularly important in terms of competitive pricing and in a new business with potential seasonality and cyclical cycles. She added that it would give some indication of the cost of idle capacity and that it would reduce the risk of the 'downward spiral effect.' As nobody really understood what she was talking about, it was suggested that, as this was only of relevance to her and the auditors, they should move on to agree the projected product costs. McGuire knew this was not the right time to pursue the matter further and, somewhat despondent, presented the cost figures that she had agreed with the relevant parties.

Based on the bill of material agreed with the design team, and after extensive discussions with McKenna, direct material was estimated at €5 per unit. As Castlegrove was heavily unionised, labour rates were based on industry norms. This resulted in a direct labour estimate of €25 per unit. This took into account the standard employer levies payable, the cost of annual leave and other labour benefits agreed with the unions. As regards overheads, McGuire had prepared a detailed analysis of each potential expense heading and classified these as either variable or fixed. Her four years experience with Castlegrove meant that she had an intimate knowledge of its cost structure. Throughout this time she had been complimented on her forecasting ability. The outcome of her analysis was that variable manufacturing overhead was projected at €30 per unit and variable non-manufacturing overhead at €3 per unit.

McGuire was fearful of raising the fixed overhead issue again, but knew that it had to be addressed. She advised her colleagues that her best estimate of the appropriate fixed overhead that should be charged to the 'Pulse' product line was €90,400 for the year. Both Holmes and Jones were adamant that they saw no basis for this charge as it would be incurred in any event and could threaten the viability of a new product that had great potential. Jones was concerned that this could have an adverse impact on the price, previously agreed, and that it could seriously undermine his sales performance. Holmes was proud of his cost control ability and did not understand why he should be responsible for costs that he had little control over. He spoke of his previous experience in Dublin where the only thing that mattered to his manager was something called 'contribution.' Jones added that it was important to have some flexibility in the application of pricing policy in the first year of a new product launch and this charge would undermine that strategy. The debate continued without any sign of reaching a consensus. It was decided to seek advice from Maloney, and he was invited to the next meeting of the project team.

At that meeting, the discussion continued in the same vein, until Maloney intervened to advise that it was important for all products to carry their fair share of overheads and if they could not, then it didn't make sense to go ahead with the project. In answer to a query from Jones, McGuire advised that €30,400 of the fixed overhead related to non-manufacturing activities and included expenses associated with his new sales office in London. Being weary of the process, all parties were relieved when McGuire reminded them that the product would make a positive contribution and was projected to record a healthy profit in the first year. She also told them, that due to the low inflationary environment generally and the excellent experience to date by Castlegrove in managing its costs, she had anticipated the same costings in 2XX7. She added that these figures could be updated during the year as part of the usual performance review process. With that, it was agreed that Somers and McGuire would finalise the proposal and submit it to the board for consideration.

Concluding Comments/Substantive Issues

As they left the meeting, Maloney emphasised to McGuire the importance of getting the overhead issue sorted once and for all, particularly as there would be more new product proposals coming to fruition in the near future. He was worried that it could lead to undue friction within the company and remembered that at a recent conference he was told that some costing systems could give rise to 'dysfunctional behaviour.' He said that he did not understand the term and added that the conference presenter noted that there are 'different systems for different purposes.' He asked McGuire, 'As there are so many different costing systems, how does one know which one to use?' She responded by saying that 'this would take some time to explain.' She went on to remind him of her previous attempts to address the overhead issue and noted that it was of particular relevance now given their intention to incentivise senior management with a bonus scheme.

McGuire assured Maloney that she would give the matter some thought and prepare a presentation for the management meeting early next month. She headed back to her office with renewed determination and began to ponder on how she would tackle the issue. She was conscious of the fact that her audience would be highly critical and would expect her presentation to focus on the specific situation in Castlegrove. In particular, she knew that any potential conflict between how they made decisions and rewarded performance would be closely watched. As she had a very good working relationship with the company auditors and was currently very busy, she decided to enlist the help of their consultancy service.

Required

As management consultant to Castlegrove, prepare a draft set of guidelines and briefing notes on how McGuire might structure her presentation to the senior management team. Your response should deal with the overall concerns expressed by Maloney and the specific issues arising from the new product decision.

Total 100 marks

Appendix 1
Projected Operating Income Statement for 'Pulse'

Period: 12 months ended	Dec 2XX6 €	Dec 2XX7 €
Revenue	467,500	552,500
Variable costs		
Variable manufacturing		
Direct material	27,500	32,500
Direct labour	137,500	162,500
Variable manufacturing overhead	165,000	195,000
Variable cost of goods sold	330,000	390,000
Variable non-manufacturing overhead	16,500	19,500
Total variable costs	346,500	409,500
Contribution margin	121,000	143,000
Fixed costs		
Fixed manufacturing overhead	60,000	60,000
Fixed non-manufacturing overhead	30,400	30,400
Total fixed costs	90,400	90,400
Operating income	30,600	52,600
Note		
Projected sales (units)	5,500	6,500
Breakeven level of sales (units)	4,109	4,109

Case 5
Spektrik plc
Falconer Mitchell, University of Edinburgh

Introduction

Spektrik plc produces and sells a range of electronic measuring devices for a variety of manufacturing applications. New products are regularly added to its range. They are devised in the Design Engineering Unit of the company by a small team of electronic engineers who all have production experience.

Competition in Spektrik's main product markets has been intensifying and over the last few years profitability has deteriorated. The chief executive has attributed this to 'an inability to control product costs as well as our key Japanese competitors have done.' He has located one cause of this problem as being 'technologically driven product design with a neglect of economic factors followed by an absence of continual cost reduction effort when the product is in production – this has led to falling product profitability over the product life cycle as prices are squeezed.'

You are a newly appointed management accountant in Spektrik plc and you have been given the task of addressing the issues raised by the chief executive. Following investigation of Japanese management accounting practice you have decided to follow the management accounting practices of your main competitors. Consequently, you have proposed the piloting of a system of target costing for the next new product launch

The Pilot Target Costing Situation

The product for which the new target costing approach is to be applied is one which will replace one of the main products in the company's product range. With the help of marketing staff you have drawn up the following financial specifications for the new product:

Product 107

1. Estimated total market life: 6 years
2. Projected sales profile:

	Product Introduction	**Product Maturity**	**Product Decline**
Duration	First three annual quarters	Next 12 annual quarters	Final nine annual quarters
Targeted unit selling price	€20	€18	€14
Budgeted sales volume for this life cycle stage	50,000 units	360,000 units	180,000 units

3. Required initial investment:

Plant & Machinery	€1,000,000
Space	€750,000
Working Capital	€250,000

4. Required return on initial investment: an average of 30% per annum.

Implementation of Target Costing Pilot

In order to implement the target costing pilot you have established a small four-man steering group comprising the heads of design engineering, production and marketing, and yourself. The group's objectives are to, firstly, specify the target cost to be set for Product 107 and, secondly, to plan how the target cost information should be used to achieve effective cost control. Finally it should make recommendations on whether and how target costing should be extended within the company.

Required

Question 1

Calculate the target cost for Product 107. This should be done on the following two bases:

(a) A single target cost applying over the whole life cycle of the product; and
(b) A set of target costs applying at each of the three stages of the product life cycle, i.e. introduction, maturity and decline.

(40 marks)

Question 2

Discuss which of the above approaches to target costing would be most appropriate in Spektrik plc.

(20 marks)

Question 3
Make recommendations on how the company can best organise to facilitate achievement of the target cost/s set.

(20 marks)

Question 4
Make suggestions on how the existing target costing implementation could be improved.

(20 marks)

Total 100 marks

Case 6
The Castleward Cycle Company
Noel Hyndman, Queen's University Belfast

Overview of the Company

The Castleward Cycle Company (CCC), a company set up in 1996 and located adjacent to the picturesque Strangford Lough, manufactures and sells a range of cycles. The company is a division of the Down Industries Group (DIG) and produces cycles that are targeted at particular specialised segments of the market. Central management of DIG has embraced decentralisation as a means of empowering local managers, controlling costs and improving profitability. Each of the divisions of DIG is judged independently on the basis of its return on investment. Having regard to the cost of capital figure used in major investment decisions, DIG has set a target of 15% for each of its divisions. Within CCC, each of the range of cycles is manufactured in separate departments, and controls and evaluations are made at this level to ensure that, overall, the 15% target is achieved.

Given the growing leisure market, and the particular expertise and reputation that CCC has developed, turnover has risen rapidly, with considerable sales growth in both Ireland and Britain (CCC's main markets). While all of CCC's sales are to external customers, there is an element of interdivisional trading within the DIG, and indeed several of the parts and components for some of CCC's cycles are purchased from other DIG divisions. Two of CCC's products are:

- The Tollymore Tourer (TT) – a specialised family, leisure cycle that provides a durable, well-equipped, value-for-money product for general road use by the occasional cyclist. The aluminium alloy cycle frame for this product is provided by another division of DIG (Eglinton Engineering and Electrical). Although the TT is viewed favourably by customers, on a price basis it has come under pressure from imported cycles
- The Donard Trekker (DT) – a high-specification, lightweight, carbon fibre framed cycle targeted at the growing number of serious mountain bikers. It is a high quality, high price product with few obvious rivals. Given the location of CCC, being near the Mountains of Mourne, it enjoys a particularly loyal following from local enthusiasts with the Donard Trekker being viewed as the brand of choice by many mountain bike aficionados.

Brian Thompson, CCC's chief executive and a keen cyclist himself, has been feted by DIG's central management as an individual who knows what it takes to be successful in this industry. However, recently, on his daily six-mile bike ride from Downpatrick to CCC's main plant, his mind has been somewhat exercised by a number of matters surrounding the production and sales of the two products described above (the TT and the DT). These are outlined below.

The Tollymore Tourer (TT) Department

The TT is produced within CCC utilising a cycle frame provided by Eglinton Engineering and Electrical (EEE), another division of the DIG. CCC does not have the authority to purchase the frame from any other source. Each TT requires a cycle frame from EEE and CCC pays EEE €80 per unit (delivered). Brian Thompson has consistently complained that the transfer price that CCC has to pay for the frame is too high and undermines the ability of CCC to achieve the target return on investment. In discussions with the central management of DIG and with David Dunlop, the chief executive of EEE, it has emerged that:

- Although EEE sells the cycle frame on the external market at €80, the department in EEE making the cycle frame is operating considerably below capacity. External sales (excluding transfers to CCC) are budgeted at 50,000 units next year.
- EEE's costs relating to the production of the cycle frame are: variable €40 per unit; fixed costs €1,500,000 per annum.
- Investment in EEE that is related to the production of the cycle frame is about €3,500,000.

Brian Thompson has produced a budget for the Tollymore Tourer department of CCC for the next year and a summary of this is shown in Appendix 1.

CCC has a more modern plant in its Tollymore Tourer department than the average in EEE and Brian Thompson has expressed concern over the comparatively low return on investment in the Tollymore Tourer department of CCC (which has resulted in a reduced overall return on investment for CCC). The fixed assets of all divisions within DIG are valued on the basis of net book value based on the historic cost.

DIG has a policy of interdivisional transfers being made at market price. Brian Thompson complains about this and, on reflecting on the situation with respect to the TT, comments, 'It's bad enough having my investment in fixed assets valued at recent (very high) acquisition costs, but having to pay such high prices for EEE's products is grossly unfair.' Thompson is particularly sensitive to these issues as he is paid a bonus on his ability to surpass the target return on investment for CCC. The higher the return on investment, the bigger the bonus. At present he is considering action to reduce the budgeted fixed costs of the Tollymore Tourer department, and hence improve the return on investment. One option is to reduce research and development expenditure in the coming year by €100,000. This could be achieved by postponing a programme aimed at improving the quality and reducing the cost (through efficiency savings) of the TT. A second option would be to reduce staff training in the Tollymore Tourer department to a level below its present budget. This would save €50,000. Both of these fixed cost expenditures are included in the budgeted fixed costs of €500,000.

The Donard Trekker (DT) Department

The DD is largely made within CCC. It is produced to a very high specification, with its frame being manufactured using reinforced carbon fibre in order to reduce weight without sacrificing strength; the frame is a critical aspect of the DT and one that gives it competitive advantage over its rivals. The revolutionary manufacturing process related to the production of the carbon fibre frame has been developed within CCC and is the envy of competitors. The Donard Trekker department has a manufacturing facility that consists of three main work stations. At present one standard model is produced, although plans have been developed to add new models to suit more specific segments of the mountain bike market. The DT is priced at €1,600.

The growth of CCC in general, and with respect to the DD in particular, has required it to institute a formal system of cost control. Brian Thompson recently commented:

> 'Modern cost control and inventory valuation procedures enhance our credibility within the group and, more importantly, have enabled us to improve our operations. Our supervisors have realised the value of good cost accounting, and the main office has, in turn, become much more aware of problems in the factory.'

Manufacturing consists basically of three processes: production of the carbon fibre frame, assembly and finishing. In the first process, all ingredients to make the carbon fibre frame are mixed before individual layers are spun and bonded using extra strength epoxy resin. Given the detailed specification, sophistication of the process and strict time requirements to produce and bond each layer of carbon fibre, frames have to be produced individually. Assembly includes hand additions to the frame, for example trekker wheels and gears, shock absorbers, sports pedals, disc brakes and a safety seat. Finishing consists of quality control checks and the packing of the cycle for dispatch. The preparation of the carbon fibre mix for the frame, while manually simple, is problematical. If the mixture contains too much or too little solidifier, it could spoil. If too little is mixed, and is therefore insufficient to complete a frame, the entire mix is lost. If too much is mixed, any excess has to be discarded. In addition, the bonding process is very precise; with the use of an incorrect amount of epoxy resin, or leaving the layers too long before compressing them, leading to frames being scrapped.

To help control the process and also provide data to evaluate performance, several months ago the Donard Trekker department developed a standard cost system with respect to the production of the carbon fibre frame (this was to be viewed as a pilot study to be used as a basis for rolling out standard costing to the whole department at a later stage). Ronnie Hurst, the supervisor in charge of the production of carbon fibre frames, and Katy Little, CCC's accountant, agreed, after lengthy discussion, a standard cost for each carbon fibre cycle frame. However, recently, after reviewing the actual performance relating to the production of the carbon fibre frames over several periods, Katy Little expressed her disappointment about the apparent lack of attention being paid to the standard costs. Data relating to the standard cost of a carbon fibre cycle frame and the most recent month's actual results are provided in Appendix 2.

Before proceeding with further analysis, Little called Hurst to arrange a discussion of variances. She also told Brian Thompson, 'Maybe we should look into an automated moulding operation. Although I haven't finished my analysis, it looks like there will be unfavourable variances again. Hurst insists that the standards are reasonable, then never meets them!' Thompson seemed disturbed and answered, 'Well, some variances are inevitable. Why don't you analyse them in some meaningful manner and discuss your ideas with Hurst, who is an expert in carbon fibre production and whose opinion I respect. Then the two of you meet with me to discuss the whole matter.'

He continued, 'While I am convinced that cost control is beneficial, it has not been the basis for our success in the past with respect to the Donard Treker department. We have always prided ourselves in being innovative, responding to customers' needs and producing high-quality products. I am somewhat concerned that when we have sorted out this standard costing system (and I am convinced we will), we might have too much focus on costs and too little focus on other factors that really bring us success.'

Required

Brian Thompson has approached Down Industry Group's central management expressing concern about the above issues. Following a forthright discussion between Thompson and Down Industry Group's central management, where all of the above facts, figures and opinions were aired, the central management of the Down Industry Group has asked you, as an independent consultant, to write a report in order to provide them with some objective views on the above and other related matters. This will help them in their deliberations. In particular, your report should include:

1. With respect to the Tollymore Tourer department:

(a) A calculation, utilising the existing transfer pricing system, of the budgeted rates of return by the Tollymore Tourer department and that part of Eglinton Engineering and Electrical producing aluminium alloy cycle frames, and a commentary on these figures.

(16 marks)

(b) A discussion of the suggestion that, as presently calculated, these rates of return figures may be misleading. On the basis of this, make recommendations as to changes in the transfer pricing and financial performance measurement systems that you feel are appropriate. If your recommendations include a change in the transfer pricing system, calculate the impact of this change on the rates of return as calculated above (assuming no change in the investment base).

(21 marks)

(c) Advice regarding: the advisability of the Tollymore Tourer department reducing research and development expenditure or reducing staff training in an attempt to improve return on investment; and the use of bonus payments to managers being made based solely on return on investment.

(9 marks)

2. With respect to the Donard Trekker department:

(a) Calculations of material, labour and overhead variances relating to the production of carbon fibre frames for the month (to the extent that they can be calculated from the information supplied). Mix variances should not be calculated.

(18 marks)

(b) An outline of the possible reasons for the variances.

(10 marks)

(c) Some pointers regarding: the accuracy of the standard costs; how standards should be set; and questions that Down Industries Group's central management might ask Brian Thompson as to how the pilot standard costs were established?

(12 marks)

3. A commentary, including specific suggestions if appropriate, on the advisability of expanding the performance measurement system to incorporate non-financial measures in the evaluations of the divisions of the Down Industry Group generally, and particularly, given Brian Thompson's comments, in the case of the Down Trekker department of the Castleward Cycle Company.

(14 marks)

Total 100 marks

Appendix 1
Summary of CCC's Budget for the Tollymore Tourer for Next Year

	Tollymore Tourer Department (CCC)
Selling price per cycle	€120
	€
Variable costs:	
Direct material	10
Cycle frame from EEE	80
Direct labour	5
Variable overhead	5
Total variable costs per unit	100
Fixed costs per annum	€500,000
Demand at current selling prices	35,000 units
Maximum capacity	50,000 units
Investment in Tollymore Tourer department	€4,000,000

Appendix 2
Standard Costs and Actual Costs for the Production of a Carbon Fibre Frame

Standard cost for a frame:

Materials	Material A	12 square metres	@	€13.50	=	€162.00
	Material B	4 kgs.	@	€25.00	=	100.00
Direct labour	Grade X	0.5 hr.	@	€13.50	=	6.75
	Grade Y	1.0 hr.	@	€13.50	=	13.50
Indirect costs	Absorb at €16.20 per frame*		@	€16.20	=	16.20

Total cost to produce a carbon fibre frame €298.45

*The normal volume of operations for overhead derivation purposes was assumed to be 450 frames per month. The estimated monthly indirect cost equation was:
Budget = €6.48 * frames + €4,374.

Actual costs (most recent month) for production of 430 frames:

Materials:
Purchased: 6,000 sq. metres Material A @ €12.50 per metre
2,000 kgs. Material B @ €26.70 per kg.
Used: 5,400 sq. metres Material A
1,900 kgs. Material B

Direct labour: Grade X 210 hrs. @ €14.06 per hr.
Grade Y 480 hrs. @ €13.50 per hr.

Overhead: Incurred €7,425

Case 7
Drumview Limited
Ciaran Connolly, Queen's University Belfast

Background

Believing that there was a market for providing good quality wooden garden and patio furniture, two sisters, Claire and Emer Grant, established Drumview Limited some fifteen years ago. After some early teething problems, the company experienced moderate growth and, by 2XX0, Drumview Limited had developed a reputation for producing products that were above average in quality and price, but not necessarily 'top of the line.'

Claire and Emer retired from the day-to-day running of the company in 2XX5, with Claire's son, Christopher, assuming responsibility for the daily management of the firm. Having worked in the company since he was a teenager, Christopher had a sound understanding of the various aspects of the business and he approached his new role with great enthusiasm and high hopes for the future. He quickly established a system of standard marginal costing and budgeting, and agreed with the management accountant that stock was to be valued at standard marginal cost for internal reporting purposes. In addition, he introduced regular management team meetings in an effort to encourage shared aims and objectives by improving information flows. The five members of the management team are:

1. The chairman of the company, Christopher;
2. The management accountant;
3. The buying manager;
4. The production manager; and
5. The sales manager.

One of the key matters for discussion at the quarterly management meetings are any variances arising between actual results and budgeted results so that any problems can be identified as early as possible and new ideas can be explored. However, after an initial burst of enthusiasm and spirit of co-operation between the other members of the management team, Christopher is now beginning to become concerned that in recent meetings the various managers seem to have become more defensive about their own positions and are not considering the company as a whole.

Products

One of the products that Drumview Limited currently produces is an eight-seater patio table and chairs. The company produces this patio table and chairs to two specifications aiming at different markets: a standard un-treated hardwood version which is sold through a catalogue; and a deluxe pre-treated pine version which is sold through independent garden centres. Production and sales of the eight-seater patio table and chairs have shown consistent growth over the past few years, and the deluxe version has become very popular in recent times. The deluxe version is currently one of the company's best selling and most profitable products and Christopher is keen to maintain market share in this product.

Production Process

Most of the company's products are made from bought-in components that are assembled by the production department. The patio table and chairs are made almost entirely from wood, except that the chairs have a fabric seat and back. The production processes are the same for both versions of the patio table and chairs, with the two products being distinguished by the type and quality of wood used. Untreated hardwood is used for the standard catalogue version, while pre-treated pine is used for the deluxe version. Both products use the same type of fabric for the seat and back of the chairs. Drumview Limited has tried to build its reputation on developing strong community relationships, and the company has a policy of using local suppliers wherever possible. Currently all purchases of hardwood, pine and fabric are sourced locally.

Quarterly Reporting

Christopher, along with the management accountant, introduced a system of standard marginal costing so that budgets could be prepared and variance analysis readily carried out. At the start of each budget period, the management accountant sends a memo to each of the three departmental managers (buying, production and selling) detailing the planning parameters for the period. Each departmental manager then responds with their outline proposals. This is followed by a period of negotiation after which the finally agreed departmental budgets are circularised to Christopher and each of the departmental managers. Christopher also receives a copy of the full master budget.

Progress against budget is discussed at the quarterly management meetings. In preparation for these meetings, the management accountant compares the actual results for the period with the planned budget and produces a variance analysis statement. Departmental managers receive details of the variances relating to their own departments and are invited to provide explanations at the management meeting. A full copy of the variance report is sent to Christopher who also attends the quarter end meetings. At recent meetings, the management accountant has begun to feel that each departmental manager holds him responsible for their shortcomings and is anxious to ensure that no blame is placed on the accounting role.

The Buying Manager

The buying manager recently warned the management accountant that the price of both hardwood and pine was due to rise in the current period. However, the management accountant did not take any account of this when setting the standard for the current period. Indeed, the buying manager believes that he has done very well to achieve the price that he has. Furthermore, the buying manager has found a new supplier for the untreated hardwood at a cheaper rate than the old supplier, but he had to make a bulk purchase to achieve this lower price. In addition, a new supplier for the fabric has also been found and the fabric has been purchased at a cheaper rate of €6.00 per chair; but as this lower price was only available for a short time, a bulk purchase had to be made.

The Production Manager

The production manager warned the management accountant that the time set for producing the eight-seater patio table and chairs was too tight, stating 'you cannot afford to make mistakes, and the men take great care handling and cutting the materials. The untreated hardwood that was purchased did not handle very well.' The production manager also told the management accountant that the increase in work rates that had originally been budgeted for was unlikely to be sufficient as the skilled labour did not like having to pack the table and chairs and therefore took longer over this, also wasting packaging. The production manager suggested that unskilled labour be hired for this purpose.

The storeman has complained about the recent bulk purchases, as he was unaware of their arrival and the storeroom is so full that it is difficult to move around safely. Furthermore, the storeman had to work overtime in order to reorganise the storeroom. He was particularly frustrated as this recent incident occurred shortly after the buying department's bulk buy of packaging materials.

The Sales Manager

During the period under review, industry prices as a whole increased. The policy of the sales department is to keep the price of the standard hardwood model slightly below that of the competition, largely because a new producer had just entered the market. In contrast, the price of the deluxe model was set higher than that of competitors in order to try and distinguish it from the rest.

The Management Accountant

The management accountant produced the budget from information given to him by the various departmental managers at the start of the period. He has a vague recollection that the buying manager phoned him to moan about prices but is confident that nothing specific was mentioned or agreed. Budgeted and standard cost information (Appendix 1) and actual results for the quarter (Appendix 2) is provided.

Required

Question 1
(a) Prepare a variance analysis statement that reconciles the budgeted profit figure to the actual profit figure for the quarter; and

(25 marks)

(b) Suggest possible causes for the variances calculated.

(15 marks)

Question 2
(a) Describe the external and internal factors which you consider would have an important influence on the profitability of Drumview Limited.

(15 marks)

(b) Discuss the information that the management accountant would need in order to take account of the factors that you have described in part (a) above. From what sources would he be able to obtain such information in his role as management accountant of Drumview Limited?

(15 marks)

Question 3
(a) Distinguish between basic, ideal and attainable standards and explain how these may be used in Drumview Limited.

(12 marks)

(b) Describe the procedure to be followed by the management accountant in formulating the budget for Drumview Limited, and discuss whether he should revise the budgets which have been already established.

(18 marks)

Total 100 marks

Appendix 1
Budgeted Sales, Production and Standard Cost Information for the Eight-Seater Patio Table and Chairs for the Quarter to 31st March 2XX6

	Standard	Deluxe
Sales price	€150	€400
Sales units	1,300	1,500
Production units	1,300	1,500

There are no stocks held at the beginning of the period.

Standard costs per unit:

Untreated Hardwood Table and Chairs — €
- Untreated hardwood (0.5 pallet @ €60 per pallet): 30
- Fabric (1 sheet): 10
- Labour (3 hours @ €8 per hour): 24
- Packaging (1 roll @ €15 per roll): 15
- Variable overheads: 18
- Total variable cost: 97

Pre-treated Pine Table and Chairs — €
- Pine (9 metres @ €10 per metre): 90
- Fabric (1 sheet): 10
- Labour (5 hours @ €8 per hour): 40
- Packaging (1 roll @ €15 per roll): 15
- Variable overheads: 30
- Total variable cost: 185

Additional Information:
Variable costs are charged on a labour hour basis.
Fixed costs for the quarter are expected to be €70,000.

Appendix 2
Actual Results for the Quarter to 31st March 2XX6

	Standard	Deluxe
Sales price	€140	€420
Sales units	1,000	1,700
Production units	1,000	1,700

Raw materials used:
Hardwood – 700 pallets @ €56 per pallet
Pine – 15,500 metres @ €13 per metre
Fabric – 2,700 sheets @ €6 per sheet
Packaging – 2,800 rolls @ €15.20 per roll

Labour – 12,000 hours @ €10 per hour
Variable overhead costs for the quarter – €72,000
Fixed costs for the quarter – €80,000

Case 8
Elveron Limited

**Barbara Flood and Bernard Pierce,
Dublin City University**

Overview of the Company

Elveron Limited is an electronic component manufacturing company based in Greystones, County Wicklow. Since its establishment by Tom Bridge 30 years ago, Elveron has manufactured components for motorcar manufacturers. However, in the last decade, due to astute strategic planning by Tom, the company expanded its product range and started to also supply truck and bus manufacturers. Elveron is now one of the largest electronic component manufacturers in Europe.

Despite the phenomenal growth of Elveron, Tom Bridge maintained a hands-on management style within the company and was regularly to be found on the factory floor packing components to complete a big order. Tom always made an effort to get to know the staff who worked for Elveron and he considers the company to have a big role to play in the local community, not only by providing employment opportunities but also by supporting local sporting, cultural and other voluntary activities. As a result of his friendly participative management approach, Tom is well liked by the hundreds of staff who have worked for the company over the years and he is much respected and admired in the local area.

David Ledger graduated from university as an electrical engineer and immediately found employment with Elveron. He has enjoyed his career with the company and has had plenty of opportunities to take on responsibility and address new challenges, such that he became head of the company's product development team in 2XX3. Another reason David has enjoyed his time with Elveron is that Tom Bridge encouraged and supported his keen interest in sailing. Since a young age, David has engaged in competitive sailing at both a national and international level, and his employer has always enabled him to work flexible hours to fit in with his training schedule. Indeed, Tom Bridge has also provided financial aid when David needed support to attend overseas training camps or faced expensive enhancement or repairs to some of his boats. In March 2XX5, David was approached to join a sailing team which was preparing to compete in the 'Around-the-world' yacht race in November 2XX5. David was obviously enthusiastic regarding this opportunity and was delighted and grateful when Elveron agreed to provide him with paid leave for the remainder of the year.

Following the race and on his return journey to Ireland in December 2XX5, David reflected that he was disappointed that his sailing adventure was over, but he was looking forward to catching up with family and friends. He knew that in his absence, there had been considerable changes in Elveron, but not having been on land for any length of time and having been consumed by his sailing activities, he was not aware of the detail. When he met some work colleagues for a drink over the Christmas holidays, they were only too happy to inform him of the changes.

Changes in Elveron

In April 2XX5, Tom Bridge's wife, Lucy, fell ill. While Lucy received immediate medical treatment and was well on the way to a full recovery by June, the incident made Tom re-evaluate his work-life balance. Consequently, he decided that he had invested enough time in his business and wanted to spend more time with his wife, children and grandchildren. Thus, he decided to sell Elveron to Cooper Inc, a US-based multi national company which is the global market leader in the vehicular electronic component market.

Cooper Inc took control of Elveron on 1 November 2XX5 and while the jobs of all Elveron employees were guaranteed for one year, a US management team, headed by Todd Lyman, has been sent to the Greystones plant to 'whip the company into shape.'

Some of the changes which were immediately introduced to Elveron by Todd Lyman and his team were as follows:

- The company has been restructured into three divisions to reflect the structure of Cooper Inc companies around the world: Car Division, Truck Division, Bus Division;
- New work practices have been introduced and production workers not only have to work in their specialised areas but must also be willing to substitute into a variety of other roles;
- Local suppliers have been replaced with Cooper Inc 'preferred suppliers,' who are typically based in Asia.

David Ledger, having listened carefully as his work colleagues recounted the story of change at Elveron, commented: 'Well that all sounds very dramatic, but I don't think it will affect me or the product development team too much.' His colleagues laughed hysterically and said 'Oh, we forgot to mention, Todd disbanded the product development team and you have been reassigned.'

Truck Division: Financial Performance January – March 2XX6

On returning to work on 2 January 2XX6, David is informed by Todd Lyman that his new role is as general manager in the Truck Division and that the company has high expectations for enhanced performance in the division in the months ahead.

Todd comments: 'David, I'll be straight with you. Things have not been going well in the Truck Division since we took over. There seem to be inefficiencies and quality problems in the production process and the staff seem to be careless and unmotivated. We expect you to sort things out as soon as possible.'

Although David has never worked previously in general management, he sets about his new role with enthusiasm. While he has to learn on his feet and encounters many hiccups, he feels that he has developed a good understanding of the division's activities by the end of March 2XX6. He is also pleased that he has won the support of staff. However, his satisfaction is shattered when he receives, via email, a 'Performance Report for the Truck Division for Quarter 1 2XX6' (Appendix 1). David was not involved in the budget setting for his division and was not aware that quarterly performance reporting had been introduced and so is frustrated to receive the report unexpectedly. From a quick review of the report he is shocked to see that it portrays the performance of the division in a negative way and that there has been no attempt to analyse or explain the variances calculated. While he was aware that a budgetary control system was used by Elveron when Tom Bridge was in charge, he does not remember it being used in such an authoritarian, constraining way. He resolves to develop his understanding of best practice in budgetary control.

As David has little prior experience of financial performance review, he decides to request the assistance of one of his friends who is a consultant specialising in management control systems. To assist his friend during the consulting process and to enable detailed variance analysis, he gathers together as much information as he can regarding the financial and operating activities of the division in the first quarter of 2XX6. This information is set out in Appendix 2.

Additionally, he feels that he will be able to seek advice from his consultant friend regarding a couple of other labour issues which have caused some difficulty in the division in the first quarter, details of which are provided below.

Labour Issues

Rate and efficiency standards

David is acutely aware that Todd Lyman has a negative perception regarding production workers, as he feels that the workers are not well motivated and their laziness is the root cause of negative efficiency variances.

David is not convinced that Todd's assessment of labour inefficiency is appropriate. In his new role as divisional manager and to enhance his knowledge and understanding of the operation of the division, David has spent many days on the factory floor in the first quarter of the year. From this experience, he has a sense that workers are actually putting considerable effort into their activities and do not appear to be obviously inefficient. Thus, he has concerns regarding the accuracy and appropriateness of the labour standards and so he gathered information about revisions to standards that, with hindsight, should have been implemented for the first quarter of 2XX6 (see Appendix 3).

Remuneration schemes

Todd Lyman is determined to change the behaviour of production workers and has suggested that he will change their remuneration scheme from a time-based scheme to some form of incentive scheme. David is concerned about how the workers may react and wants to gather relevant information before approaching Todd to discuss the issue further. He has compiled remuneration data regarding a typical production worker (Appendix 3) and is seeking advice on the implications of the potential change.

Required

You are the consultant who has been recruited by David Ledger and are required to write a report that addresses the following issues in the Truck Division:

Part 1

(a) Discuss the problems which you consider exist in the budgetary control system operated by Elveron in the first quarter of 2XX6 and particularly outline the flaws which you consider are present in the form and content of the Performance Report which was issued to David Ledger concerning the Truck Division.

(18 marks)

(b) Describe, with explanation, the changes which you think should be made to the form and content of the divisional Performance Report in order to improve its effectiveness as a management control tool.

(10 marks)

Part 2

(a) For the Truck Division in the first quarter of 2XX6, prepare a statement which reconciles the static budget gross profit to the actual gross profit, showing the revenue and cost variances in as much detail as the available information permits. (Note: do not use the information in Appendix 3 in answering this requirement.)

(28 marks)

(b) Provide a commentary to accompany the statement prepared at (b)(i), which outlines the potential reasons for the occurrence of the variances calculated.

(14 marks)

Part 3

(a) Describe the potential impact of inaccurate labour standards in the Truck Division and outline a process to determine the accuracy of the revised standards proposed by David, as set out in Appendix 3.

(8 marks)

(b) Utilising the revised standards set out in Appendix 3, calculate planning and operating labour rate and efficiency variances and reconcile the static budget labour cost to the actual labour cost for the Truck Division for the first quarter of 2XX6. Briefly interpret your calculations.

(7 marks)

Part 4

(a) Prepare a schedule which compares the weekly wages that would be earned by John Murphy under the existing time-based scheme and the two possible incentive schemes at the following weekly activity levels:

- 1,000 components manufactured
- 1,300 components manufactured
- 1,600 components manufactured

Indicate, with reasons, which scheme you think might be preferred by the workers.

(8 marks)

(b) From the company's perspective, outline the potential benefits and drawbacks of introducing an incentive-based remuneration scheme for the production workers in the Truck Division.

(7 marks)

Total 100 marks

Appendix 1
Truck Division: Performance Review

MEMO

To:	David Ledger, General Manager, Truck Division
From:	Todd Lyman, CEO, Elveron
Date:	5 April 2XX6
Re:	Quarterly performance review

David,

You will find below the performance report for your division for the first quarter of 2XX6. In line with Cooper Inc's group management control system, you will receive such a report within five days of every quarter end. You have one week to respond in writing to the report.

As you will see from the report, the performance of your division has been poor in the quarter under review, with operating profit falling short of budget by over 36%. Costs appear to have escalated out of control and we are particularly concerned with the cost of labour. We thought the new work practices would improve things and reduce costs, but things appear to be getting worse not better and it may be that a round of redundancies in November will provide the best long-term solution to whip the work force into shape.

We look forward to receiving your report by the 12th.

Todd.

Truck Division
Performance Report – Quarter 1, 2XX6

	Budget	Actual	Variance
Sales and production units	70,000	85,000	15,000
	€	€	€
Sales revenue	420,000	501,500	+81,500
Materials	49,000	78,795	-29,795
Production labour	89,250	123,088	-33,838
Manufacturing overhead (variable & fixed)	138,250	165,367	-27,117
Gross profit	*143,500*	*134,250*	*-9,250*
Divisional non-manufacturing costs	25,000	21,000	+4,000
Allocation of central Elveron costs	15,000	22,000	-7,000
Allocation of Cooper Inc. HQ costs	21,000	39,000	-18,000
Divisional operating profit	*82,500*	*52,250*	*-30,250*

Appendix 2
Truck Division: Operating Data for Quarter 1 2XX6

The standard cost sheet for the component manufactured by the Truck Division shows the following:

	€	€
Selling price per unit		6.00
Materials:		
Material X: 100g @ €4 per kg	0.40	
Material Y: 50g @ €6 per kg	0.30	0.70
Labour:		
Grade I: 3 minutes @ €10 per hour	0.50	
Grade II: 2 minutes @ €12 per hour	0.40	
Grade III: 1.5 minutes @ €15 per hour	0.375	1.275
Manufacturing overhead:		
Variable: 6.5 minutes of labour-time @ €9 per hour	0.975	
Fixed: €1 per component	1.00	1.975
Total manufacturing cost		**3.95**
Standard gross profit per unit		**2.05**

The annual budget for the Truck division for 2XX6 was based on achieving sales of 280,000 units in the year which, considering the estimate of the industry size in Europe, would provide a market share of 20%. At the end of the first quarter for 2XX6, the latest information indicates that the size of the European market is ahead of expectations by 10%.

At 1 January 2XX6, there were 1,000 kgs of Material X and 1,000 kgs of Material Y in stock in the division. During the first quarter, 13,000 kgs of Material X and 6,500 kgs of Material Y were purchased and at the end of the quarter 2,950 kgs and 1,550 kgs respectively, remained in stock. Due to the inexperience of a new staff member who is responsible for the stock accounting records, the purchase prices for both materials have not been recorded separately. Since the purchase of the company by Cooper Inc, it is the Truck Division's policy to maintain a stock of finished goods at each quarter end amounting to 5,000 components.

The mix of labour set out in the standard cost sheet above is the optimum mix for the manufacture of the component. However, due to the new work practices introduced since Cooper Inc took over the company, staff are required, when directed, to complete the work normally done by another grade. It should be noted, however, that regardless of the nature of the work completed by the worker, he/she is paid for the time at the rate at which they were originally recruited and for which they are trained. In the first quarter of 2XX6, the actual time worked by employees recruited at the three different grades and the actual rates of pay were:

Grade I:	3,980 hours @ €9.80 per hour
Grade II:	3,400 hours @ €11.76 per hour
Grade III:	3,000 hours @ €14.70 per hour

Appendix 3
Truck Division: Labour Issues

1. Labour standards

Having observed the activities of the workers in the Truck Division and spoken to the supervisors and the division's process engineers, David considers that the labour standards for the Truck Division should have been revised in the first quarter of 2XX6 as follows:

Grade I:	2.85 minutes @ €9.80 per hour	€0.4655	
Grade II:	2.30 minutes @ €11.76 per hour	€0.4508	
Grade III:	2.10 minutes @ €14.70 per hour	€0.5145	€1.4308

2. Remuneration schemes

John Murphy is a typical employee working at the Grade II level within the production function of the Truck Division. He is currently paid at a rate of €11.76 per hour and works a standard 40-hour week. During the first quarter in 2XX6 he worked an average of six hours overtime per week (employees cannot work more than ten hours overtime under the company's work-life balance policy), which was paid at time and a half.

Possible new incentive schemes proposed by Todd Lyman:

1. Piece-rate with guaranteed minimum
Grade II workers would be paid at a rate of €0.36 per good component manufactured and there would be a guaranteed minimum of €380 per week.

2. Differential piece-rate
Grade II workers would be paid as follows:

Up to 1,300 components per week:	€0.34 per component
1,301–1,500 components per week:	€0.39 per component
1,501+ components per week:	€0.45 per component

Note: Todd assumes that under both of these schemes, employees will work faster, facilitating all production within the available work time.

Case 9
Autoparts SA
Tony Brabazon and Tony O'Dea,
University College Dublin

Overview of the Company

Autoparts SA is a large diversified French firm operating in several countries. Total sales for the year ended 30 April 2XX7 were €535 million with profits before tax of €58 million. Its primary activities concern automobile and truck sales and repairs. The stated strategy of the firm is to grow through acquisition. Early in 2XX7, following a review of the group's activities, it was decided to search for potential acquisition targets in the fast-growing Chinese market. Shortly afterwards in February 2XX7, two subsidiaries were acquired. The first subsidiary, Varin pte, operates a large chain of truck maintenance depots in China. The second acquisition, another Chinese company, Yatese pte, produces a range of generic truck spares. These are typically installed on trucks during repairs once the truck's warranty period has expired.

A variety of management and staff incentive schemes are in operation throughout the group. At present, the incentive scheme operating in the two new subsidiaries has two components (these schemes were in existence before the subsidiaries were acquired by Autoparts SA). The first component of the scheme is a bonus pool which is calculated as described in the two paragraphs below. The calculated bonus is paid to managers in two instalments, half at the end of the year in which the bonus is earned and half one year later. For example, if a bonus is earned in the financial year ended 30 April 2XX7, half of this is paid shortly after the year end, the remaining half would be paid in May 2XX8.

Varin

The truck repair market in China is highly competitive. Varin aims to provide a premier service and this has been successful in attracting a loyal, stable, customer base. The entire management team share in a bonus pool which is calculated annually, based on 10% of profit before taxes and bonus. Non-management staff do not receive a bonus, but in order to encourage staff loyalty and good morale, the salaries paid to non-management staff are approximately 10% higher than those offered by similar employers in China.

Yatese

The generic truck spares produced by this subsidiary are sold to repair depots across China. The company has established a reputation as a supplier of reliable, low-cost spares. Although sales are currently limited to the domestic market, the board of directors of Autoparts SA is currently considering a proposal to make a substantial investment in Yatese to allow it to expand its sales overseas. The management team of Yatese share in a bonus pool calculated as 10% of gross profit, having deducted the cost of the bonus in the calculation of gross profit.

In addition to sharing in the management bonus pool, the general manager of each subsidiary is paid an extra bonus of €30,000 once the return on capital employed (ROCE) of their subsidiary exceeds 22%. ROCE is calculated as:

$$\frac{\text{Profit before interest, tax and all managers' bonuses}}{\text{End of year book value of net assets}}$$

The following financial information relating to each of the two subsidiaries has been provided:

	Varin	Yatese
Book value of assets at 30 April 2XX7:	€000	€000
Buildings	500	2,000
Machinery and equipment	200	2,000
Net current assets	2,100	2,600
Capital employed	2,800	6,600

	Varin	Yatese
Year to 30 April 2XX7:	€000	€000
Sales	4,000	5,500
Raw materials	1,200	1,000
Direct labour	1,500	2,300
Gross profit	1,300	2,200
Management compensation	300	350
Other costs	100	450
Profit before tax	900	1,400

Note: The abbreviated profit and loss accounts above do not include any expense for management bonuses. Fixed assets are currently being depreciated on a straight-line basis over their remaining life of 20 years (all fixed assets are currently being depreciated). The depreciation cost is included in 'other costs'.

You are also supplied with the following information:

(1) A post-acquisition valuation of the assets of the two subsidiaries revealed that buildings are undervalued by 100% on the above balance sheets, machinery and equipment is overstated by 10% and a deduction of 5% should be made

from net current assets to reflect irrecoverable debts. Although these adjustments have been made for the purposes of preparing group consolidated financial statements, they have not been reflected in the books of either subsidiary as shown above. During the revaluation process, it was estimated that the residual life of the assets averages ten years.

(2) Divisions with a similar business risk elsewhere in the group are expected to earn a ROCE of 30% in the case of Varin and 25% in the case of Yatese.

The chief executive officer (CEO) of Autoparts SA has asked the chief financial officer (CFO) to investigate the current bonus schemes of each of the two subsidiaries. In turn, the CFO has asked you to undertake a preliminary analysis. The CFO has suggested that the revised bonus scheme could consider including a share of general head-office overheads in measuring the profitability of the two subsidiaries. He commented that 'these costs are incurred for the benefit of all the subsidiaries in the group, and each of them should pay their fair share.'

Required

Question 1
Calculate the total bonuses in respect of each of the divisions for the year just ended (30 April 2XX7):

(a) Using the existing book asset valuations
(b) If the assets are revalued, using the information in note 1 above, *with effect from 1 May 2XX6*.

(30 marks)

Question 2
Critically evaluate the current bonus scheme from the viewpoint of both the group and the subsidiary management teams.

(20 marks)

Question 3
Comment on the CFO's suggestion that the profitability of each of the subsidiaries should be measured after they have been allocated a share of general group administration costs.

(20 marks)

Question 4
Outline a suggested compensation plan for the management teams of both divisions. Your suggestion must:

(a) Defend the scheme you have chosen outlining both its strengths and weaknesses; and

(b) Include a sample calculation of the bonuses payable to each division's management team under your chosen scheme.

Clearly state any assumptions you make in presenting your calculations.

(30 marks)

Total 100 marks

Case 10
IXL Limited
Joan Ballantine, Queen's University Belfast

Overview of the Company

IXL Limited has been engaged in the automotive industry for some 20 years and is now specialising in the manufacture and sale of components for heavy goods vehicles. The company operates from a number of sites located throughout the UK and the Republic of Ireland. For accounting purposes, each site has been set up as an investment centre with responsibility for both profits and return on capital investment. The company's head office is based in the Republic of Ireland which enables it to benefit from low levels of corporation tax. IXL Limited's customers represent some of the world's major manufacturers of heavy goods vehicles who are located throughout Europe.

During its history, IXL Limited has been a profitable company holding a respectable share of the market for automotive components. More recently, however, IXL Limited's financial performance has been poor relative to that of its competitors. At a board meeting in late 2XX5, the finance director, John O'Leary, presented the financial results of the company which showed the company's continual financial decline in terms of both sales volume and profitability.

You are employed as the financial controller within IXL Limited and your immediate boss is John O'Leary. As part of your on-going education, you are undertaking a Master of Business Administration (MBA) at a prestigious UK university. To this end, your studies have provided you with useful insights into the problems of running a profitable business. Lately you have been giving the problems within your own company some thought and you are of the opinion that some of the problems which IXL Limited currently faces are as a result of poor management of working capital, in particular stock management. In the past you have shared some of your concerns with the finance director.

The finance director, John O'Leary, has responded to your concerns by recently attending a high profile conference in Europe devoted to the issue of stock management. During a number of presentations, enterprise resource planning (ERP) systems were reported as being instrumental in enabling organisations to effectively manage their stock levels and bring about improvements in revenue generation. On his return, John O'Leary asks you to investigate the concept of ERP systems as a potential solution to the problems which IXL Limited is experiencing. Your search leads to the identification of a software package, SAP ERP Automotive Supplier Packaged Solution, which its vendors (SAP AG) suggest is a fully integrated solution for improving business processes and boosting competitive advantage. The promotional material for the SAP ERP Automotive Supplier Packaged Solution states the following:

> *'Far too often, companies lose valuable time and money because business units must customise IT solutions. This cripples your ability to support customers and facilitate expansion. To unlock business value and make information work for you, you must align and standardise your processes across critical business areas. This is what the SAP® ERP Automotive Supplier Packaged Solution can do for companies like yours. Offering the most complete solution of industry-specific best practices available, the SAP ERP Automotive Supplier Packaged Solution supports your business processes up and down the supply chain – from start-up orders to sales orders delivered via electronic data interchange (EDI) right down to production planning and control.*
>
> *The SAP ERP Automotive Supplier Packaged Solution delivers comprehensive documentation and configuration information for use in many industry-specific scenarios that help promote user buy-in, simplify project management, and quickly implement optimised business processes. Right out of the box, this packaged solution serves as the foundation for daily customer interaction and execution in many areas, including material requirements planning, inbound delivery, goods receipt, production, delivery note creation, shipping, billing documents, and invoice creation and settlement.'*

When you report your findings to the finance director he further asks you to undertake an analysis of the potential benefits of implementing a SAP ERP Automotive Supplier package within one of IXL Limited's manufacturing sites based outside Dublin, which would subsequently act as a pilot site for the remaining manufacturing sites should implementation be successful.

The Dublin Site

The Dublin site is currently managed by Jack Duggan, an MBA graduate. Jack has recently taken over management of the site from John Forsythe who was general manager for the past 18 years. Jack Duggan is keen to adopt new working practices in order to improve the site's efficiency. The site currently manufacturers one main component which it exports to a small number of major European manufacturers of heavy goods vehicles.

After a number of meetings with Jack Duggan, you ascertain that the ERP package would have the greatest potential for improvement when used as the basis for reorganising business processes and adopting a just-in-time (JIT) system. The adoption of the ERP and JIT manufacturing system would enable the Dublin site to respond to customer demand more promptly, thereby providing them with a competitive advantage leading to increased sales volumes over the next five years. The adoption of the ERP system would also enable the production manager to manage stock more effectively. These changes would, however, necessitate modifications to the factory layout, which would involve significant capital investment in production machinery. On the negative side, the increased sales volumes arising as a result of the implementation of the ERP system would need to be managed carefully by the Dublin site. Indeed, you are already aware that the Dublin site has in the past found it very difficult to effectively manage their accounts receivable.

After a detailed review of the existing costs and benefits of the Dublin site, you ascertain the costs and benefits of implementing the SAP ERP system as per Appendix 1.

The estimates in Appendix 1 have not taken account of reduced stock holding costs as a result of implementing the JIT system. Historically the Dublin site has had a poor reputation in terms of managing stock levels. However, the recently appointed Jack Duggan is convinced that initial cost savings are likely to be in the region of €250,000 and that these savings will rise by 5% per annum each year over the next five years. Finally, your estimates do not include the loss of rental income which is currently received by the Dublin site from leasing out its spare capacity to a third party. Jack estimates that the current rental income of €600,000 per annum will be reduced to zero by equal amounts in the next three years starting in 2XX7.

You have been asked by the finance director to evaluate whether the board of directors should support the implementation of the ERP/JIT system within the Dublin site. Decisions of this nature have historically been made by IXL Limited on the basis of return on investment (ROI) which is currently set at a level of 22%. However, the finance director, aware that you are studying for an MBA, is giving you considerable freedom to use additional methods of appraisal which you feel might be more appropriate in arriving at a decision. In preparing your report you should be aware that the finance director will require you to clearly define any technical 'jargon' you use.

The company's cost of capital is currently 8%.

Required

Question 1

Prepare a report to the finance director advising whether or not IXL Limited should go ahead with the ERP/JIT project. You should use methods of appraisal which you consider to be appropriate given the time frame of the investment. However, since these are likely to be novel to the finance director, you should provide a brief overview of each additional method of appraisal used. You can ignore taxation and inflation in your analysis. Please state clearly all assumptions you have made in your calculations.

(40 marks)

Question 2
The finance director has in the past heard you state that ROI is an inappropriate method of appraisal when used as the only means of making investment decisions. You are required to outline the problems associated with using ROI and to suggest how the alternative methods of appraisal you have used in part (a) help alleviate these.

(20 marks)

Question 3
During your evaluation of the ERP/JIT project, you ascertain that risk might be an issue which needs to be addressed. Explain to the finance director the importance of risk and how it might be reflected in the appraisal you have carried out.

(10 marks)

Question 4
You are also aware of the dangers of ignoring taxation and inflation when appraising capital investment projects using discounted cash flow techniques. Your report should consider how the calculations you have undertaken in Question 1 would need to be adjusted to account for tax and inflation. (Recalculations are not required).

(10 marks)

Question 5
What actions need to be taken by the Dublin site to ensure that it manages accounts receivable arising from the extra sales volume in an effective manner?

(20 marks)

Total 100 marks

Appendix 1
Anticipated Financial Benefits and Costs of Implementing the SAP ERP Automotive Supplier Package Solution

Financial Benefits:

As a result of adopting a JIT system it is anticipated that additional sales over the next five years will be as follows. The selling price of the component manufactured at the Dublin site will remain at its current level of €380:

Year	Additional Sales of Components
2XX7	40,000
2XX8	45,000
2XX9	50,000
2X10	52,000
2X11	48,000

Financial Costs:

Manufacturing Costs

The variable manufacturing cost of each component is as follows:

Direct Labour	€107
Direct Materials	€85
Variable Overheads	€50

The fixed manufacturing overheads associated with the extra volume of production are estimated to be €900,000. However, when output increases beyond 49,000 additional components this will necessitate additional supervisory costs and annual fixed manufacturing costs will rise by a further €250,000.

Non-manufacturing Costs

Variable selling and distribution costs are estimated to be €30 per component, while the fixed selling and distribution costs are expected to be €250,000. However, it is expected that the fixed selling and distribution costs will be step fixed in nature, with the result that these will increase by €125,000 when additional sales exceed 45,000 components, and a further €85,000 when sales exceed 50,000 components.

Additional fixed operating overheads of €100,000 will be charged to the Dublin site as a result of implementing the ERP/JIT systems. The €100,000 represents overheads incurred by the corporate function. It is the company's policy to allocate such overheads to the manufacturing units on the basis of the unit's ability to bear.

In addition to the above costs, you ascertain the following:

Costs incurred to date on the ERP/JIT project to employee specialists to determine cost/revenue estimates	€50,000
Cost of purchasing and implementing SAP ERP Software	€1,500,000
Capital cost of production machinery	€6,000,000
Resale value of production machinery after five years	€150,000
Depreciation of production machinery (straight line basis)	€1,200,000 per annum
Amortisation of software costs (straight line basis)	€500,000 per annum

Case 11
Lennon Department Store Limited
**Bernard Pierce and Barbara Flood,
Dublin City University**

Introduction

Deirdre Lennon had been in the business long enough to know that major decisions may be required in the near future. As she walked down the corridor, she reflected on the fact that the meeting with her senior management colleagues had been tense and difficult – an all too familiar experience these days. Although the company had managed to maintain a modest increase in turnover, she was very conscious that margins were being squeezed, competition was increasing and predictions of a looming crisis might be closer to reality than some of her colleagues liked to believe. She reflected on the decision just taken by senior management to engage a firm of consultants to examine various aspects of the business and to recommend a strategy for the future. As she left her office that evening, Deirdre tried to imagine how the original founders of Lennon Department Store might have reacted in the circumstances. 'I just wonder how they would have coped with these conditions' she thought, as she pondered the origins of the company.

Background

John and Emer Lennon returned to Ireland over 50 years ago, having emigrated to England ten years earlier. A small amount of personal savings, supplemented with funds generated from the sale of a family inheritance, presented an opportunity to acquire a small retail outlet in the suburbs of Dublin for the equivalent of €8,500.

The location was well known to John and Emer and seemed to offer several advantages as a location for a small newsagent and general store. The surrounding area seemed set for significant housing development and was well served by public transport routes, being close to a train station and major bus routes. The particular site offered many attractions, being located on a corner between a major road and a quiet cul de sac. The main building was in a dilapidated state and refurbishment and fitting out required some bank borrowings, but it offered a generous amount of space for the business and also provided modest upstairs accommodation for the Lennons and their young family. A further attraction was a small yard and some outside sheds, which the Lennons quickly realised provided scope for future expansion.

Although the initial years presented many challenges and much hard work, it became clear at an early stage that the business offered major potential for development and Lennon's shop became well established, not only as a well stocked retail outlet, but also as a social venue and recognised meeting place. Within a few years, the family moved to a new home and the store expanded to fill the available space. A major decision was required when the Lennons were offered the then astronomical sum of the equivalent of €900,000 by an international hotel chain who wished to purchase their premises and build their first hotel in Ireland.

Overcoming sentimental attachment, the Lennons finally accepted a slightly higher offer and invested the money in two larger and more modern outlets, one of which would be the responsibility of their eldest daughter, Deirdre. A few years later, Lennons opened two further stores, continuing the strategy of seeking out areas of high housing density, within easy reach of urban commuters. A combination of sound business knowledge and shrewd financial management ensured that Lennon's stores continued to trade successfully and, about 20 years ago, a majority shareholding was sold to an investment consortium and Lennon Department Store Limited was subsequently formed. Deirdre Lennon, who had almost 20 years' experience in the business and had built up an excellent reputation with suppliers, was appointed chief buyer in the company. Her younger brother, Seamus, continued in his existing role as manager of one of the stores and John and Emer retired from the business.

Under new management, the company persisted with the strategy of controlled expansion, while continuing the Lennon tradition of carrying a full range of stock and seeking to locate stores in city centre locations, shopping centres and densely populated neighbourhoods near major suburban commuter routes. The company now operates department stores and supermarkets at 25 locations throughout the country. It is centrally managed from a head office building, but also has a manager and support staff at each location.

Details of Current Business

The company sells a wide range of products and, to facilitate more effective management, has classified its products into the following merchandise groups:

Group 1	Hardware products
Group 2	Ladies' fashion wear
Group 3	Men's fashion wear
Group 4	Children's wear
Group 5	Concession sales
Group 6	Supermarkets

Concession sales arise where the company has entered into an agreement that the concession owner may sell their products in specified stores and pay Lennon Department Store Limited on a monthly basis a specified commission based on sales value. Where a concession agreement exists, staff are employed by the concession owner and Lennon Department Store Limited has no responsibility for payroll costs.

Store Details

Although the company has followed a consistent strategy regarding store location, variations in traffic patterns, competition and housing development mean that demand for Lennon's products varies greatly. Consequently, it would not be appropriate to establish all stores of the same size and Lennon has three different store sizes, which it categorises as follows:

- Category A Offering all product groups listed above, including a supermarket on site.
- Category B Offering product Groups 1 to 5, but excluding a supermarket.
- Category C Offering only Group 1 products.

In order to standardise the offering as much as possible, all stores within each category are exactly the same size, i.e., all Category A stores are the same size, all Category B stores are the same size and all stores within Category C are the same size. The company measures size in terms of square footage as shown in Appendix 1.

In addition, within each category of store the same amount of space is allocated to each group of products and they are located in exactly the same position within each store. Decisions regarding these issues are taken at head office, as are decisions regarding suppliers, purchasing conditions and selling prices. Management take the view that the Lennon reputation and brand is critically dependent on the implementation of company policy. Local management is responsible for ensuring compliance with these policies and for maintaining the high level of customer service associated with the Lennon name.

Management Information System

The company has a well established management information system and monitors key performance indicators on a daily, weekly and monthly basis. Cost and revenue behaviour patterns for year ending 31st December 2XX7, together with other relevant data, are outlined in Appendix 1 and the board has requested a projected profit statement for the year, based on this information and on further relevant details set out below.

Sales are monitored daily – in absolute terms, by comparison with budgets, and also on the basis of sales per square foot. The VAT rate on the company's products is predominantly 21%, with the following exceptions. Children's wear for children below age 10 has 0% VAT rate, so a blended rate of 10% is used for children's wear. For supermarkets, because of the different products at different rates, the blended rate is about 8%.

Gross profit margin is defined as the VAT-exclusive selling price of an item less the cost of that item. For Group 5 (concession sales), commission is treated in the same way as gross profit. The gross profit margin is calculated daily per product by the IT system, by taking the selling price of the item from the cash registers and comparing it with the cost price of the item which is held in the product data base.

Payroll costs are monitored weekly and are accumulated for the week and expressed as a percentage of VAT-exclusive sales. Overheads are monitored monthly from management accounts and totals expressed as percentage of VAT-exclusive sales.

Depreciation is not included in overheads, but shown under a separate heading. Properties are all owned by the company and are not depreciated. The company has a standard fit-out cost per store and this is depreciated on a straight line basis over seven years.

All central costs are accumulated for head office and charged to the stores as a percentage of VAT-exclusive sales.

Proposals Under Consideration

The consultants that have been engaged by Lennon have been requested to advise on two specific areas where proposals are being considered for year ended 31st December 2XX7. From a detailed analysis of cost behaviour, the consultants have concluded that the cost information set out in Appendix 1 is accurate and reliable for this level of activity. They have also advised that because of company policy to maintain a high degree of autonomy between product groups, a significant amount of payroll and overhead costs are committed for a lengthy period and should therefore be considered fixed for the purpose of changing levels of activity. These amount to 30% of payroll and 35% of overhead projected for the coming year and it is recommended that this information be used in calculating the financial impact of any proposed changes in activity levels or space allocation.

Proposal 1:

Management is considering the possibility of discontinuing the supermarket business and devoting the space currently occupied by supermarkets to increasing the space available for Group 1 business. It is expected that such a move may result in some reduction in the number of customers frequenting the store, referred to in the business as footfall, and that this is likely to have some adverse impact on the level of business. There is some uncertainty regarding what this impact will be, and estimates vary from a possible decrease of 1% in projected turnover (probability 15%) to a decrease of 3% (probability 60%) or, in a worst case scenario, to a decrease of 8% (probability 25%). Management would like to see an appropriate analysis that incorporates these estimates. Because of the difficulties in estimating the impact on footfall, management would also find it helpful to know what will be the critical level of footfall if proposal 1 is implemented, i.e., what percentage reduction in footfall could occur before profits fall below existing levels. Any reduction in demand is expected to apply uniformly to all sales of all product groups in the stores involved.

Proposal 2:

A separate proposal has been put forward to be considered independently of proposal 1. Commercial director, Thomas Reilly is proposing that space in every store be allocated to product groups in a way that maximises the company's annual profits, subject to 25% of the space in every store being devoted to concessions and a maximum of 25,000 sq. ft. being allocated to any one product group. A further requirement is that a minimum of 10% of space in each store will be allocated to each product group, except that Category B stores will not have supermarkets, and Category C stores will only have hardware and concessions. Concessions in Category C stores are expected to show the same levels of profitability as those in Category B stores.

Deirdre Lennon reflected on the meeting just ended and how she had voiced her opposition to both proposals. She had expressed the view that the company should continue with the growth strategy that has been the foundation of its success, arguing 'I have a hunch that our bigger stores are proportionately more profitable and we therefore need to grow our stores as rapidly as possible. If we introduce concessions into our smaller stores, then the Lennon brand will very quickly become diluted and future growth potential compromised. Furthermore, we should continue the policy of stocking the full range of products with uniform allocation of floor space. This has been the foundation for Lennon's success.'

As she left her office that evening, Deirdre wondered why her senior management colleagues seemed slow to support her position.

Required

You are required to present the following in the form of a report to the board of Lennon Department Store Limited:

1.
(a) A projected profit statement for the company for the year ending 31st December 2XX7, based on the data shown in Appendix 1 and showing appropriate analysis by store category and by product group.
(b) A commentary on the company's projected performance.

(24 marks)

2.
(a) Calculation of the financial impact of implementing proposal 1, incorporating the issues raised by management in connection with implications for footfall arising from the proposal.
(b) Your advice regarding what further issues should be considered before making a decision regarding proposal 1.

(28 marks)

3.
(a) Calculation of the effect on profitability if the company decides to proceed with proposal 2, showing the recommended space allocation.
(b) Your advice regarding what further issues should be considered before making a decision regarding proposal 2.

(28 marks)

4.
(a) Your response to Deirdre Lennon's arguments regarding strategic priorities.
(b) Your recommendations regarding the most important factors for management to consider in developing long-term strategic plans for the company.

(20 marks)

Total 100 marks

Appendix 1
Relevant Data

	Store Category		
	A	B	C
Number of stores	5	12	8
Size of each store in Sq feet	90,000	50,000	25,000
Allocation of space			
Group 1	15,000	10,000	25,000
Group 2	10,000	7,500	
Group 3	7,500	5,000	
Group 4	7,500	5,000	
Group 5	20,000	22,500	
Group 6	30,000		
Total	90,000	50,000	25,000
Sales per square foot (including VAT)			
	€	€	€
Group 1	500	500	500
Group 2	450	450	
Group 3	425	425	
Group 4	400	400	
Group 5	600	600	
Group 6	1000		
Gross profit margin			
	%	%	%
Group 1	40	40	40
Group 2	35	35	
Group 3	34	34	
Group 4	30	30	
Group 5	20	20	
Group 6	25		

Appendix 1 (continued)

Payroll as % of VAT-exclusive sales			
	%	%	%
Group 1	13	13	13
Group 2	15	15	
Group 3	14	14	
Group 4	15	15	
Group 5	0	0	
Group 6	15		

Overheads as % of VAT-exclusive sales			
	%	%	%
Group 1	16	18	20
Group 2	16	18	
Group 3	16	18	
Group 4	16	18	
Group 5	16	18	
Group 6	10		

Cost of fixtures and fittings per store	€3m	€2.2m	€1.4m	
Annual head office costs				€10m

Case 12
Top Flite plc
Joan Ballantine, Queen's University Belfast

Overview of the Company

Top Flite plc is a multinational company which operates in the USA, Canada and the UK. The company manufacturers a wide range of electronic components which it sells to a number of major electronics companies throughout the world. The company is structured along divisionalised lines with major divisions located in Chicago, Boston, Toronto, Manchester and Belfast. All of the divisions of Top Flite plc operate as investment centres with minimal interference from the head office which is based in Manchester. Historically, divisional performance has been assessed on the basis of return on investment (ROI) as this measure is widely used and accepted within the electronics industry. Divisional directors are required to report to the board of directors of Top Flite plc on a quarterly basis with respect to their performance.

Over the past five years the Belfast division has performed well in terms of ROI achieved. The financial data relating to the Belfast division is presented in Table 1 below.

Table 1
Belfast Division – Top Flite plc

	2XX1 € million	2XX2 € million	2XX3 € million	2XX4 € million	2XX5 € million
Invested capital	550	535	500	440	390
ROI	5.45%	5.98%	6.60%	6.82%	6.92%

ROI is calculated using divisional net profit divided by invested capital (after accounting for depreciation). Divisional net profit is arrived at after deducting central overheads which are charged to the divisions of Top Flite plc on the basis of the divisions ability to bear such costs. Since 2XX0, the Belfast division has been consistently charged central overheads equal to 4% of its invested capital.

The Belfast division is currently in the process of developing its three-to-five year plan. As part of the planning process, the finance director has asked managers within the division to submit capital investment proposals. To date a number of proposals have been submitted. Three of these proposals have been classified as 'significant' projects when compared to the division's current level of invested capital. Data relevant to the three proposals is presented in Appendix 1. Capital investment proposals within the divisions of Top Flite plc have historically been evaluated on the basis of ROI and each division is set an overall target ROI against which its performance is evaluated. The Belfast Division's target ROI has been 6% for some years now.

The appropriateness of using ROI as the primary measure of performance has recently been the subject of debate at the head office of Top Flite plc. The debate has been fuelled by the chief executive officer (CEO) of Top Flite plc who earlier in the year attended a high profile seminar in the US, hosted by Robert Kaplan and David Norton, on the balanced scorecard. At the seminar, the limitations of using ROI were outlined and the advantages of adopting a multi-dimensional balanced scorecard approach as a strategic management system were discussed. In addition, the advantages of adopting alternative financial measures of performance such as residual income (RI) were also outlined. On his return from the seminar, the CEO is keen for Top Flite plc to investigate the possibility of implementing alternative performance measures such as RI and/or a balanced scorecard approach within the entire organisation. In the interim, he has suggested that the basis for comparison of performance between divisions should be a controllable figure, where central overheads are to be excluded from the calculation of ROI. Additionally, he has suggested that the company investigate implementing a measure to either complement or replace the use of ROI. For the purposes of calculating RI, Top Flite's cost of capital of 6% should be used as the basis for the charge for capital.

The finance director of the Belfast division is aware that the implementation of a balanced scorecard approach within the division could have a signficiant impact on the way that performance is assessed by Top Flite. However, within the Belfast division, there is currently very little knowledge concerning the balanced scorecard concept.

You are employed as the financial controller of the Belfast division. Your boss, the finance director, is aware that you are undertaking your accounting examinations and he asks you to prepare a report which investigates the implications of adopting alternative measures of performance such as those outlined above. In particular, he has asked you to undertake the following:

Required

Question 1
Analyse the historical performance of the Belfast division using the data presented in Table 1 above. Comment on the ROI trend and any issues this raises.

(10 marks)

Question 2

Analyse the historical performance of the Belfast division using the data set out in Table 1 on both a controllable ROI and RI basis. Explain clearly the rationale for using a controllable figure for your calculations and comment on any issues raised by the results.

(20 marks)

Question 3

Appraise the viability of the three independent capital projects currently being considered by the finance director of the Belfast division using both the ROI measure and the proposed residual income measure. You are required to consider the performance of each project on a year by year basis. Which of the projects would the finance director be likely to accept if he adopts a short-term or a long-term perspective? Would the decision reached by the finance director be congruent with the decision made by adopting a company perspective?

(Note: In evaluating capital projects the division normally charges depreciation on a straight line basis over the life of the asset which in the case of all three projects being currently considered is four years. You should use the beginning of year asset values for the purposes of calculating yearly ROI and residual income measures).

(40 marks)

Question 4

Outline the concept of the balanced scorecard and how it might be used as a strategic management system within the Belfast division.

(15 marks)

Question 5

Discuss the key issues that the Belfast division would need to consider in advance of getting involved in the design and implementation of a multi-dimensional performance measurement system such as the balanced scorecard.

(15 marks)

Total 100 marks

Appendix 1
Belfast Division: Top Flite plc
Capital Investment Projects

	Project A € million	Project B € million	Project C € million
Initial cash outlay on fixed assets	-80	-80	-80
Net cash inflows in year 1	28	25	22
Net cash inflows in year 2	15	18	20
Net cash inflows in year 3	15	22	25
Net cash inflows in year 4	15	27	35

Case 13
Mississippi Inc.
Tony Brabazon and Tony O'Dea, University College Dublin

With a weary sigh, Jeff Essos sat back in his chair. It was six p.m. on a sunny Saturday evening but he reckoned that he'd be lucky if he got home before 11 p.m. Ever since he had co-founded Mississippi Inc. with his ex-classmate, Rachel Rosenthal, two years earlier, the work had been hard and the hours long, but generally Jeff had enjoyed the challenge. As Rachel has remarked when they founded the firm, with Jeff's accounting and finance skills and her marketing skills, they were bound to succeed!

Mississippi Inc. was a fast growing e-business, specialising in direct sale to consumers of both books and CDs. The firm made all its sales to customers over the Internet and followed a marketing strategy of offering low prices, a wide product range and a nationwide three day delivery promise. The customer would place an order on the firm's web-site, paying for the goods purchased with his or her credit card. The order would then be sent to the firm's distribution centre where all stocks were kept, and the order would be picked from stock, packed in a cardboard box and then shipped directly to the customer.

The day before, Jeff had received the latest financial report from his assistant, Barney Shuter. Sales were continuing to grow rapidly and, while the firm was far from profitable as yet, Jeff consoled himself with the thought that Mississippi Inc. was the dominant e-retailer in the market and that the current losses were partially arising because of the firm's heavy expenditure on advertising which was considered necessary in order to build a strong customer base. A more immediate problem which concerned Jeff were the high costs arising in the distribution depot of the firm. In earlier months, the rapid growth in sales had placed severe demands on the firm's distribution depot, and delivery times to customers had started to slip. Consequently, the depot had been significantly expanded last month and many of the activities of the depot had been automated. The good news was that the new depot was working smoothly and had sufficient capacity for at least the next six months, even taking into account the expected rapid sales growth. The bad news was that the costs of the distribution depot had increased substantially as a result of the expansion, which was somewhat surprising given that the efficiency of the warehouse had improved due to the increased level of automation.

In the past week, Jeff had been contacted by a major freight carrier (USP Inc.) who had offered to undertake the entire distribution function for Mississippi. USP's proposal was that Mississippi would pass the customer order directly to USP Inc. who in turn would provide their own warehouse facilities (stocked with Mississippi inventory) and staff, and would be fully responsible for picking, packing and shipping the order to the customer. In return for this service, USP would charge Mississippi a flat 8% commission on gross sales revenue (for example, if the value of goods shipped to customers in a given month was €10 million, USP would receive a commission of €800,000).

Jeff was considering this proposal but was uncertain as to whether the activities of the distribution depot should be outsourced to USP. Although the decision was a complex one, Jeff thought that it would be useful to start by comparing the financial implications of each alternative. Luckily, Mississippi had implemented an activity-based costing system in its distribution depot the previous year, so Jeff thought that much of the necessary information would be readily available.

Last month, sales to customers were €10 million with an average sales order value of €50 (200,000 individual sales orders last month). On average last month, each order contained two items; so an order could be for two books or perhaps one book and one CD. The key costs associated with the activities of the distribution depot were as follows:

Activities	Activity Cost Driver	Activity Cost Driver Rate
Picking	Number of individual items	€1.25 per item
Packing	Number of individual items	€0.25 per item
Preparation of shipping documents	Number of orders	€0.75 per order
Transfer to shipping area	Number of orders	€0.50 per order

Jeff knew that an activity cost driver rate was not a 'true' variable cost but rather contained both a fixed and a variable component. The fixed component of each of the above activities was as follows:

Activities	Fixed Cost Component (€) Per Month
Picking	400,000
Packing	80,000
Preparation of shipping documents	100,000
Transfer to shipping area	80,000

Based on sales projections developed by the marketing department, it was expected that sales would increase by 30% in Euro terms in each of the next two months. Customer loyalty to Mississippi was known to be strong and because a high number of customers would be 'repeat' customers, it was expected that for the next two months the average order value would be €65 and that the number of items would increase to an average of three per order. Fixed costs are not expected to increase next month but are expected to increase by 10% at the start of the following month.

Note: In answering the following requirements, the following simplifying assumptions can be made:

(i) If the decision is taken to outsource the operations of the distribution centre, the centre can be closed down immediately and all costs associated with the activities of the distribution centre can be immediately avoided by Mississippi.
(ii) Stock-holding costs will not change if the operations of the distribution centre are outsourced.
(iii) Presently, customers pay the shipping charges of their orders and these charges are not included in the sales figures above. This practice will not change if the operations of the distribution centre are outsourced.

Required

Question 1
Calculate the estimated cost of operating the distribution centre for each of the next two months.
Clearly show your workings and clearly highlight (and defend) any assumptions you make in your calculations.

(20 marks)

Question 2
Calculate the estimated cost, for the next two months, of outsourcing the activities of the distribution centre to USP.

(15 marks)

Question 3
Assuming that the fixed costs of all the non-distribution activities of Mississippi are €4,000,000 per month and that the average total variable costs per order (excluding variable distribution depot costs) are 80% of the selling price of the order, calculate the level of sales required to break even next month if the distribution depot activities are outsourced to USP.

(20 marks)

Question 4
Critically evaluate the proposal to outsource the activities of the distribution centre to USP.
Your answer should consider both the financial and non-financial implications of the proposal.

(20 marks)

Question 5

Jeff Essos is concerned that the current budgetary control system of the firm may be providing inadequate information to senior managers. He is considering implementing a balanced scorecard.

Design a balanced scorecard, suitable for presentation to senior managers on a monthly basis. Your scorecard should clearly indicate the perspectives and related measures you consider important for Mississippi Inc. and should defend your choice of perspectives and measures.

(25 marks)

Total 100 marks

Case 14

EasyONline

Tony Brabazon and Tony O'Dea,
University College Dublin

Overview of the Company

Ghodrat Moghadampour founded EasyONline, a chain of cyber-cafés, three years ago. The cafés provide 24 hour on-line access to the Internet, as well as selling a range of drinks and snacks. From an initial, single, café in London, the chain has grown to 21 cafés, spanning major cities in several European countries. With heavy tourist traffic in many major European cities, and only a 31% home PC penetration rate in several key European countries, the potential for sales growth seems assured for the immediate future. Sales in the current year are expected to be €50 million.

Despite this success, Ghodrat is puzzled by the latest month's financial report. Despite adding five new cyber-cafés to her growing chain during the month, and a stable customer volume at existing cafés, the financial report showed a small reduction in the chain's profitability. Ghodrat is concerned by this development as the business plan calls for an initial public offering (stock market listing) in eighteen months time, and she wants to be able to show a record of consistent, annual, profitable sales growth. She holds half of the equity in EasyONline. One quarter of the equity is held by a major PC supplier.

EasyONline competes against existing cyber-cafés by providing a top-quality service at a low price. Each café is large, typically in excess of 100 square metres, and is stocked with the latest PC models with flat-screen displays. Each café has a dedicated, high-speed optic fibre connection to the Internet. Costs are minimised due to the economies of scale that EasyONline is able to generate. For example, the cost of each café's high-speed net connection is reduced on a per-user basis because the café is open 24 hours per day. To ensure high utilisation of its cafés, EasyONline usually targets, high 'footfall' locations in the centre of cosmopolitan towns and cities which have both a large domestic and a large tourist population. Average weekly traffic for established cafés is approximately 30,000 customers per week. Each location has a standard design which reduces outfitting costs.

Café revenue arises from several streams. The user pays a 'flat-rate' fee for computer usage, currently €1 for 30 minutes computer use. The time is rounded up to the next half hour, thus a user spending 40 minutes on-line pays €2. The cafés sell a range of drinks and snacks and also generate revenue from printing services and sales of diskettes and CDs. During the past three months, EasyONline has launched a pilot programme in three of its cafés which generates revenue from advertising. The customer base, primarily 16 to 35 year olds, is attractive to advertisers. A limited amount of on-screen advertising has been sold, and advertising space on walls and mouse-mats has also been sold. The pilot scheme has been successful and will be extended to the entire chain of cafés in the next month.

Following an examination of customer records, it has been found that a typical customer stays on-line for 25 minutes between 9 a.m. and 6 p.m., and for 48 minutes outside these times. Peak log-in times are typically between 3 p.m. and 7 p.m. but these vary between countries. For example, the chain's Spanish cafés show high traffic from 7 p.m. to midnight.

To date, EasyONline has operated a variety of café sizes, but no attempt has been made to determine the 'optimal' size of café in each country. Ghodrat feels that some of the cafés are the 'wrong' size and are losing money. If a café is too small, it is hard to recover the fixed costs of both staff and the high-speed Internet connection. If the café is too large, it suffers from low utilisation, resulting in excessive lease (rent) and internet connection costs. The following information has been collected from two cyber-cafés in the UK:

(i)

	Manchester	London
Number of computers	200	600
Average monthly number of customers	40,000	180,000
of which:		
customers during 9 a.m.–6 p.m.:	12,000	80,000
customers during 6 p.m.–9 a.m.:	28,000	100,000

(ii) *Staff costs:*
Each outlet must have at least one employee present 24 hours per day. This costs €120,000 per year. Previous cost studies have found that variable staff costs are approximately 10% of total revenue earned in the café.

(iii) *PC costs:*
A major PC supplier holds an equity stake in EasyONline and supplies PCs to EasyONline under a revenue sharing agreement. Under this agreement, EasyONline do not buy the computers in their cafés but pay the PC supplier a 'rental' of 10% of the computer usage fees earned in each café.

(iv) *Lease costs:*
Leases are generally for five-years. The current annual lease costs for the cafés are €240,000 for the Manchester café and €3,600,000 for the London café.

(v) *High-speed Internet connection costs:*
These costs are similar in all major UK cities, and depend on the amount of bandwidth (capacity) required. This is largely determined by the number of computers in the café. Bandwidth can only be supplied in discrete amounts. For cafés with up to 300 computers, the cost is €15,000 per month. For 300 to 700 computers, the cost increases to €35,000 per month.

(vi) *Other costs:*
General administration and overhead costs per café are comprised of a fixed element of €5,000 per month and a variable element of 5% of total café revenue.

(vii) *Non-computer usage revenue:*
The pilot advertising programme operates in both the London and Manchester cafés. In each café, the non-computer usage revenues (sales of drinks, snacks, printing services, diskettes, CDs and advertising) are 40% of total revenue earned in the café. The contribution margin on these sales is 70%.

Required

Question 1
Calculate the average total monthly revenues earned in both the London and Manchester cafés.

(15 marks)

Question 2
Calculate the number of half-hour blocks of computer time (the 'product') that must be sold each month in order to breakeven in the Manchester café.

(20 marks)

Question 3
Calculate the monthly profitability of both the London and Manchester cafés if customer numbers:

(a) Remain at current levels;
(b) Increase by 10%.

Note: Assume that the customer mix (9 a.m.–6 p.m. vs. 6 p.m.–9 a.m.) remains unchanged when calculating **3(b)** above.

(20 marks)

Question 4

Considering the café chain's cost structure (fixed versus mixed) and other relevant information in the scenario, list two plausible reasons why the chain's profitability may have dropped last month.

(20 marks)

Question 5

Ghodrat is unhappy with the current 'flat-rate' pricing system of €1 for 30 minutes net-access. She feels that this flat-rate pricing strategy encourages excessive use of the café at peak times such as mid-afternoon, and underutilisation of the café at off-peak times.

Suggest alternative pricing strategies for the cyber-café.

(25 marks)

Total 100 marks

Case 15
Beara Bay Cheese
Margaret Healy, University College Cork

Introduction

Jana Williams established Beara Bay Cheese, located three miles outside Durrus in West Cork, as a commercial vehicle through which to market her highly popular farmhouse cheeses. Initial research and test marketing was highly favourable. Based on this favourable response, Jana expanded production beyond that anticipated in her business plan – with difficulty, given the long lead times required for maturing and ripening the cheeses. However, the annual results for the current year are disappointing and far below Jana's expectations (see Appendices 1 and 2):

> 'Somehow things never seem to work out like the business plan says – I know the basic product works … this year, we even made more cheese than planned – and managed to sell it all and could have sold much more – but I never seem to hit the profit numbers that I expect.'

Beara Bay Cheese

Beara Bay produces two products: CaiseBui and BearaBeag. CaiseBui is a gouda-style hard cheese with a rich milky flavour. It is made from cows' milk and takes six months to mature. BearaBeag is a semi-soft table cheese, also made from cows' milk, and it ripens in one month. Both products are extremely popular, with demand outstripping supply in the marketplace. Jana currently assumes full responsibility for managing the production facility, as well as marketing and distributing the finished product.

Linking production to anticipated future sales demand is a tricky balancing act for Beara Bay. Given the length of time required for maturing the cheeses and the amount of storage space needed for this stage of the process, Jana is anxious to expand the production volumes of each product. Currently there is excess physical capacity at her premises. However her 'feel' for the potential of such expansion does not seem to be reflected in the financial results and she is at a loss as to how to explain why:

> 'I just don't get it … the process is simple … the cheeses virtually sell themselves … All I have to do is get them to the marketplace – this year I made

many more kilos of cheese than I needed for just to simply breakeven. Where has all this extra revenue gone from the profits figure?'

Days spent delivering and selling the cheeses are also taking Jana away from the production process, and she is thinking about focusing solely on supplying the catering trade:

'I know I could easily sell a lot more cheese ... I just don't seem to have the time to make it, what with all of the time and effort that goes into getting the product to the customers... Don't get me wrong – I love the customer interaction and the banter of the country markets – I just don't seem to have time to do everything I want to do.'

The Sales Process

Beara Bay cheeses are packaged in two kilogram blocks. The waxed cheese is first placed in a protective plastic sleeve and is then boxed into distinctive, pre-printed rectangular shaped wooden boxes. The cheese is sold through two distribution channels: to the catering trade, via fortnightly deliveries; and direct to the consumer via farmers markets in Midleton (150 mile round trip) and Bantry (20 mile round trip). Because deliveries to the catering trade are only scheduled once a fortnight, Jana frequently has to make unexpected trips to customers requesting extra cheese. Despite the disruption this causes, Jana is slow to change the current practice of not charging extra for such deliveries:

'The catering trade is my 'bread-and-butter' ... they have always wanted more cheese than I could supply and I no longer even need to go out looking for business... The farmers markets may be just a passing fad, so why change the way I do business in the one marketplace I can rely on.'

During the past year, Jana has invested heavily in consolidating her presence as a supplier of high quality cheeses. €10,000 was spent employing a marketing consultant to develop an advertising campaign for the Beara Bay brand in the catering sector. As part of this process, a company web-site was developed and is due to go on-line shortly.

The Management Accounting System

The accounting system at Beara Bay Cheese is, at best, rudimentary. The basic unit of analysis is 'per kilogram of cheese.' Overheads, consisting of all expenses other than the direct materials and direct labour used in the cheese making process, are allocated to each of the products based on the kilograms of cheese produced. In the current year, for example, overheads were expected to amount to €67,200; planned sales level was 12,000 kgs of cheese; thus the overhead rate used by Jana in drawing up the business plan was €5.60 per kg. Retail price per kilogram of cheese was then calculated based on a required mark-up of 20% for CaiseBui and

40% for BearaBeag. Using this information, Jana calculated the budgeted breakeven level of sales to be just over 7,100 kilograms of cheese, as shown below:

Contribution per kg of cheese sold	=	€113,360 / 12,000 kg
	=	€9.45 per kg
Breakeven sales level	=	€67,200 / €9.45 per kg
	=	7,111 kgs of cheese.

The overhead allocation process at Beara Bay is very simple: the accountant explained the objective as being that of apportioning overheads to units of product – so Jana has done just that. Closer investigation has yielded further information. Production-related overheads (30% of total overheads) consist largely of those costs relating to storing the cheeses during the ripening and maturation phase. The greater the amount of time taken for this process, the higher the cost. Details relating to marketing-related overheads are in Appendices 3 and 4. It has been suggested to Jana that she use this additional information to install a more sophisticated activity-based costing system.

Thom's Proposal

Jana's son Thom is interested in getting involved in the business on a part-time basis and has approached her with a proposal. He is aware of his mother's growing frustration with the 'accounting numbers' and has begun to research the area in an effort to gain her confidence in his ability. Thom has come to the conclusion that focusing on the contribution margin and breakeven level of sales is simply focusing on maximising short-term profits from the marketplace:

> 'I believe the business should ignore the short term in favour of a longer-term view: we need to increase our market penetration and profits will follow … that breakeven calculation is useless anyway … all it does is give an estimate of how much cheese to produce – but then provides no clue as to how much of each *type* of cheese.'

Thom is interested is acting as an agent for the Beara Bay brand, initially on a part-time trial basis. Under the terms of his proposal, Thom would purchase BearaBeag cheese from Jana, at a pre-agreed price, for re-sale at a new Cork-city based farmers market held in the car park of a major shopping complex where Thom is convinced that there is a clear demand. Thom intends to purchase the cheese direct from the Beara Bay ripening sheds. He does not require the cheese to be placed into wooden boxes. Instead, it will simply be double-wrapped in protective plastic, thus reducing the packaging cost to 10% of its current level. All subsequent sales expenses become Thom's responsibility; however Jana as producer remains liable for any customer complaints and product returns. Revenue foregone resulting from unsold stock is Thom's responsibility. Jana is unsure about the proposal, both in light of the current profitability levels of the company and her removal from direct contact with the customer.

Thom has identified a number of costs involved in his proposal. He will need to pay an annual registration fee of €300 to join the market and an annual levy, currently €100, to cover the public liability insurance premiums for the market. The round trip from Durrus is 130 miles. Thom intends expensing this mileage at the same rate as that used by Beara Bay Cheese (€0.40 per mile). The market is run once a week, every week of the year. The purchase of a display stand and weighing scales for selling the cheese will cost Thom €520. Thom intends to sell the cheese on a per weight basis, charging €19 per kg. He estimates the annual cost of packaging supplies to be €800. Jana has indicated that if the proposal goes ahead, the maximum amount of product she could make available to Thom for the coming year would be 1,200 kgs of BearaBeag. Doing so, however, would mean there would not be enough production in the short term to service the current levels of demand for all existing customers. Thom anticipates earning €2,500 from this project. Jana is not willing to sell the cheese for less than €14 per kg.

Required

Jana and Thom have yet to make a decision regarding the future development of Beara Bay Cheese. They have identified two issues to be addressed. There are concerns regarding the adequacy of the current management accounting system. Jana is also unsure as to whether Thom's proposal is viable for either Thom or Beara Bay Cheese. They have approached you as an independent financial consultant and, having made all of the above information available to you, they now await your advice and recommendations.

Your report to Jana and Thom should include consideration of the following matters:

1. With respect to the existing management accounting system:

(a) Using the figures in the business plan, review the budgeted breakeven level of sales calculated for Beara Bay Cheese. In your answer, include a commentary on the figures previously provided by Jana.

(15 marks)

(b) Discuss the relevance and limitations of breakeven analysis to business decisions at Beara Bay Cheese.

(15 marks)

(c) Determine the profitability of each of the customer groupings identified by Jana, based on the actual costs provided for the year and using principles of activity-based costing. Round all calculations to the nearest whole number. Comment on these figures.

(15 marks)

(d) Advise regarding the suitability of an activity-based costing system for Beara Bay Cheese. Comment on how such systems assign indirect costs to cost objectives. Should Jana continue using the existing simple cost system or should Beara Bay install a more sophisticated activity-based costing approach?

(25 marks)

2. With regard to Thom's proposal:

(a) Determine the maximum price Thom should pay, and the breakeven sales revenue and units, if his agency proposal is to earn its target profit. Comment on the implications of accepting Thom's proposal. Include in your answer an estimated calculation of the financial consequences for Beara Bay.

(15 marks)

(b) Advise Beara Bay Cheese on the advisability of expanding the business via the agency proposal. Include specific suggestions as to any other options that may be available, or that should be considered.

(15 marks)

Total 100 marks

Appendix 1
Extract from Business Plan

Beara Bay Cheese
Budgeted Profit and Loss Account for the year ending x/x/xx

	CaiseBui	BearaBeag	Total
Turnover	€75,600	€119,560	€195,160
Direct materials	15,000	21,000	36,000
Direct labour	20,000	25,200	45,200
Contribution	**40,600**	**73,360**	**113,960**
Net profit	12,600	34,160	46,760

Appendix 2
Actual Figures

Beara Bay Cheese
Profit and Loss Account for the year ending x/x/xx

	CaiseBui	BearaBeag	Total
Turnover	€89,400	€144,500	€233,900
Direct materials	18,600	34,000	52,600
Direct labour	22,980	28,050	51,030
Contribution	**47,820**	**82,450**	**130,270**
Net profit	3,420	19,550	22,970

Appendix 3
Market-related Overhead Costs

Activity	% of total
Packaging[1]	10
Travel	35
Advertising[2]	15
Product promotions[3]	3
Cost of late orders	5
Administration[4]	32

Notes:

1. There was no opening stock of boxes and there were 261 boxes in stock at the end of the current period.
2. Advertising costs largely relate to the marketing campaign aimed at the catering trade, although the additional cost of recipe sheets for distribution to customers at farmers markets is also included here. This cost is split evenly between the two markets.
3. Costs recorded here relate to 'taster' cheese samples provided free to customers at the farmers markets and are allocated based on the percentage of cheese sold at each market. 75% of the cost related to the BearaBeag product.
4. Administration overheads include market registration charges as follows:
    a. Midleton market €250 per annum.
    b. Bantry market €100 per annum.
   Beara Bay Cheese employs a part-time book-keeper (Sandra Cronin). She has recommended that her salary of €15,000 per annum, currently included in the Administration cost pool, is best spread across product or customer profitability calculations proportional to turnover. The remainder of the administrative overheads relate to the costs of sales dockets and are allocated based on the number of transactions in each market place.

Appendix 4
Customer Transaction Details

	Midleton market	Bantry market	Catering trade
Sales in kgs:			
CaiseBui cheese	1,700 kgs	300 kgs	4,000 kgs
BearaBeag cheese	2,000 kgs	1,000 kgs	5,500 kgs
Average size of transaction	0.25 kgs of cheese	0.20 kgs of cheese	20 kgs

Case 16

Newtown Manufacturing Limited

Tom Kennedy, University of Limerick

Overview of the Company

Power Corporation plc is a major supplier of boilers, power generation equipment, components and related support services worldwide. It was organised around product groups, each with its own manufacturing facilities. In 2XX5, it made a strategic decision to purchase Newtown Manufacturing Limited from its founder John Grimes, rather than develop a greenfield site. Grimes was a self-trained engineer with many years experience in a similar business in America and had accumulated sufficient capital to realise his life-long ambition of returning to Ireland and setting up his own business. He did this ten years ago by setting up Newtown Manufacturing to supply boilers and components to the Irish and European market. The timing was ideal in that it coincided with the beginning of the economic boom in both Ireland and the UK. Grimes recognised that he did not have the requisite managerial skills to run a business and hired Joe Scanlan as general manager. He formed an excellent working relationship with Scanlan and allowed him to strengthen the managerial team to support the continually developing and successful business. He recognised the excellent performance of the management team by allocating them 15% of the equity in 2XX2.

In 2XX5, after serious deliberation with his family and the other shareholders, Grimes decided to accept a very attractive offer for the business from Power Corporation plc. The terms agreed meant that Newtown would continue to trade independently and Grimes would work in a consultancy capacity for a minimum of five years. The senior management of Newtown would be retained and aggressive performance targets were agreed. At that time, Newtown Manufacturing employed 160 people in a plant on the outskirts of Dublin. It operated two shifts a day for five days a week. Since the takeover by Power Corporation, Newtown had been restructured into two distinct product groups: boilers and components. Each group had control over the manufacturing, engineering and sales/distribution of its products. They were supported by a small general management team in Ireland and were to make a contribution to corporate services and support.

Business Performance/History

Newtown Manufacturing was profitable from the beginning. By the time it was sold to the Power Corporation in 2XX5, its turnover was €15 million and its return on investment (ROI) was in the order of 8%. Power Corporation senior management had identified Newtown as a well-run organisation with untapped potential. It was particularly interested in its components business and had developed a strategic plan that would result in a significant investment in that area. Power Corporation had been impressed with the quality of the products presented by Newtown at a number of trade shows. It had come to the conclusion that it could double its components business in five years and earn a minimum of 15% ROI. It was confident that it could achieve major changes in its operating systems and capitalise on the modern computer-integrated components manufacturing facility commissioned by Newtown in 2XX4. It planned to phase out the manufacturing of boilers at Newtown and service this business from its Munich plant, where it could achieve much greater economies of scale.

The overall market for components had increased dramatically in the last few years and Newtown had capitalised on that situation, particularly in the UK. It had built a reputation as a quality and reliable supplier. It had phased-in new technology and updated its product range in response to customer demands. It had made a strategic decision to invest in the development of a range of highly specified products for the aerospace industry. It manufactured these products in its Gamma product line and was extremely proud of its position as market leader. However, it had come under very severe pressure recently from its largest UK customer to reduce the basic selling price of this range of products or risk losing the business to another supplier. The issue became even more acute when Scanlan and Grimes visited the 2XX6 Birmingham trade show and learned that a competitor was now offering similar products from its newly commissioned Malaysian plant at 10% below Newtown's best price. Scanlan and Grimes took immediate action on their return by asking Bill Durkan, the finance manager, to investigate the situation as a matter of urgency. They knew that they would have to be well prepared before briefing the senior management at Power Corporation and were concerned about the performance targets that they had agreed during the takeover process.

Current Accounting System

Durkan ran a very tight operation. He was a competent accountant and had developed an excellent working relationship with the auditors and company bankers. He concentrated primarily on the company's statutory financial reporting requirements and the cash management of the business. He freely admitted that he had not the time or the expertise to introduce a more sophisticated system of accounting for managerial reporting, costing or control purposes. Monthly accounts were available within five working days of the end of the month. They consisted of a standard form of profit and loss account with year-to-date comparison against budget. The cost of sales figure was calculated by making the necessary adjustments for inventory movements.

The monthly accounts were supplemented by a product line performance report. This showed the accumulated direct costs and a statement of general overheads. It was produced by using a traditional job costing system. The actual results for the first three months of 2XX6 for the components product lines are shown in Appendix 1.

Product costs were used to help determine individual product prices, assess product profitability and, occasionally, make product mix decisions. Actual direct material and direct labour were charged to individual jobs and accumulated by product line. Overhead was grouped under four headings, as shown in Appendix 1. A single overhead rate per direct labour hour was calculated to allocate the general overheads to each product line. The resulting overhead was added to the actual direct costs to determine the total product cost. Newtown's overall aim is to achieve a mark-up of approximately 20%. It allows for some discretion in terms of discounts and special offers. This strategy has worked well for Newtown since its inception. It has consistently achieved growth rates of over 10% in sales volume and profitability in the last five years.

Durkan had been concerned for some time about the integrity of the cost information and the need to reflect the changing cost profile of the organisation. He was conscious of the significant shift in the labour mix from direct to indirect, and the impact that this would have on the overhead rate been used for pricing purposes. He knew that the trend of introducing more technically sophisticated plant and services would continue. As Newtown had no difficulty retaining its existing customer base to date, and continued to grow its market share, the issue was not deemed a high priority. However, recent feedback from its sales people and an urgent telephone call from Scanlan meant that the issue had to be addressed now. Durkan met with his recently recruited financial analyst, Mick Dowd. They discussed the potential benefit of using different overhead rates and the possible impact on individual product costs. They reviewed expenditure by department and the available operating activity by product line. In both cases, performance was in line with budget. They noted that the actual overhead recovery rate for the components group was €39.16 per direct labour hour for the first three months of the year versus a budget of €40. They were happy that the direct costs were competitive and would continue on the expected downward trend year on year. Finally, they decided that the best course of action was to analyse how the general overheads expenditure was incurred, as it was approximately 60% of its total costs.

Dowd has previously worked as part of an implementation team with a large banking company who adopted activity-based costing (ABC). He convinced Durkan that the situation at Newtown was particularly suitable for the application of the ABC principles and process. Durkan had heard about ABC at a conference some years ago and had only a vague understanding of it. He remembered the speaker saying that 'overhead should not be viewed as a cost to be added to direct material and labour. Rather, one should focus on the activities performed by the support departments and try to link the cost of performing them to the products.' Durkan told Dowd he would look at his conference notes, if he could find them, and do some background reading on the subject. He knew that he needed to get the full co-operation of Grimes and the senior management team in order to make the task feasible. He expected resistance from some of them whose only interest was in the introduction of the latest manufacturing technology and a reduction in the money spent on administration.

Product Costing Review Strategy

Durkan was proud of the job he had done at Newtown and his careful financial management was recognised as a major factor in its success. As he was not familiar with the ABC process, he did not wish to undermine his position by promoting investment in such a system at this stage. He decided to present a case to the senior management that suggested changing circumstances had undermined the ability of the current system to allocate a 'fair share of overheads' to individual products. He would remind them of the basis for using the traditional direct labour hours allocation method and the benefit of looking more critically at what was happening now in order to allow them make a better assessment of how much each product was contributing to the bottom line. He would emphasise the steps he had taken to ensure that the direct material and labour costs were accurately recorded and assigned. He would recommend the carrying out of a pilot study in the components product group using other allocation methods. He would tell them of the potential benefits of refining the existing costing system and applying the ABC principles. He would commit to reviewing the outcome of the study with them before deciding on the next step. He would promise to give them some background information on the ABC system and an overview of its key attributes and features. He would emphasise that the pilot study would be largely driven by his financial analyst, Mick Dowd, but would require some co-operation from them. He knew that he would have Scanlan's full support for this strategy, particularly given the feedback from the Birmingham trade show.

After a robust debate, the Newtown senior management team agreed to support Durkan's strategy. The decision was greatly helped by the news of the competitive threat to the Gamma product range. Durkan was mandated to critically review the components product group cost structure and see if Newtown could or should revise its pricing policy.

In carrying out the brief, Durkan and Dowd decided to initially concentrate on the first three months of 2XX6. Dowd was freed up from his day-to-day duties to concentrate fully on the project. His initial ambition to trace some of the general overhead directly to the individual product lines gave rise to too much confusion and was quickly abandoned. In conjunction with Durkan, he identified the key data that was required and the process that was likely to succeed. He interviewed each support department head so that he could reclassify the main categories of general overheads into more homogeneous expense headings. This iterative process facilitated the identification of the key tasks or activities that were being performed by each support department. Dowd had learned from previous experience that it was critical to set a realistic limit on the number of activities chosen. In consultation with Durkan, he decided not to exceed 20 for the pilot study.

During the process of activity identification, Dowd also decided on the operational measure or driver that best reflected the use of that activity. This decision reflected the best attempt at identifying a cause-and-effect relationship between the activities chosen and the costs incurred. The choice of driver was also influenced by the ability to capture the relevant information in an economically feasible manner. The process stimulated much debate and was underpinned by the assumption that being approximately right was acceptable. The outcome of this stage of the process is presented in Appendix 2. Durkan and Dowd were confident that they had the information necessary to estimate a revised and much more credible product-costing model.

Concluding Comments

Both Durkan and Dowd were delighted with the degree of co-operation and communication developed by the exercise. Michael Doyle, the manufacturing manager, noted that it was great that manufacturing and accounting people were having an intense discussion about resources. He expected the study to clearly demonstrate what a tight ship he was running. Richard Davies, the sales/marketing manager speculated on the possibility that this exercise would confirm his assertion that manufacturing productivity had stalled in the last year and that it was no surprise that Newtown was under competitive threat. Larry Williams, the engineering manager was enthused by the expectation that his efforts to reduce the number of engineering charge orders would be vindicated and that Grimes`s personal agenda could no longer block progress in this area. For his part, Durkan was confident that he now had a solid basis for his argument with Davies to be more discerning in his choice of customers and the need to achieve better economies in the delivery of its products.

Required

Question 1

Prepare revised product-costing models for the components product group, based on the information available.

(20 marks)

Question 2

Comment on the outcome of the revised costing models, with particular reference to the competitive position of the Gamma product line.

(40 marks)

Question 3

Advise on whether Newtown should adopt ABC.

(20 marks)

Question 4

In order to assist Durkan in making his presentation, prepare a brief set of notes setting out the circumstances in which you would expect ABC to be most beneficial and summarise its key attributes and essential features.

(20 marks)

Total 100 marks

Appendix 1
Components Group: Product Line Performance Report

(Traditional Job Costing System using Direct Labour Hours): January–March 2XX6

	Product Lines (Gross)				Rate per direct labour hour *1	Product Lines (Unit)		
	Alpha €	Beta €	Gamma €	Total €		Alpha €	Beta €	Gamma €
Sales value	1,600,000	1,650,000	1,150,000	4,400,000		80.00	110.00	115.00
Direct costs								
Direct material	400,000	255,000	250,000	905,000		20.00	17.00	25.00
Direct labour	220,000	225,000	135,000	580,000		11.00	15.00	13.50
Total direct costs	620,000	480,000	385,000	1,485,000		31.00	32.00	38.50
General overhead								
Manufacturing	265,392	298,565	199,043	763,000	13.27	13.27	19.90	19.90
Engineering	98,435	110,739	73,826	283,000	4.92	4.92	7.38	7.38
Sales & distribution	192,522	216,587	144,391	553,500	9.63	9.63	14.44	14.44
Administration	226,783	255,130	170,087	652,000 *2	11.34	11.34	17.01	17.01
Total general overhead	783,132	881,021	587,347	2,251,500	39.16	39.16	58.73	58.73
Total Product Cost per Traditional System (Direct labour hours)				3,736,500		70.16	90.73	97.23
Profit by product line/unit (Before inventory adjustments)	196,868	288,979	177,653	663,500		9.84	19.27	17.77
				Mark-up 18%		14%	21%	18%

*1 Total direct labour hours 20,000 22,500 15,000 57,500
*2 Includes contribution of €130,000 to Corporate head office
Volume (units) 20,000 15,000 10,000 45,000

Appendix 2
Components Group: Major Activities and Cost Drivers for First Three months of 2XX6

		Cost Driver Volume by Product Line						
Activity	Cost Drivers	Alpha	Beta	Gamma	Total	Total €	Dept.	Total €
1 Mould design/manufacture	no. of parts-square foot	20	35	35	90	325,000	Mnfg	
2 Manufacturing operations	no. of machine hours	20,000	26,250	22,500	68,750	233,000	Mnfg	
3 Supervision of direct labour	no. of direct labour hours	20,000	22,500	15,000	57,500	120,000	Mnfg	
4 Quality inspection	no. units audited	40	50	55	145	85,000	Mnfg	763,000
5 Plant engineering/utilities	square feet	12,000	7,500	9,000	28,500	157,000	Eng	
6 Process and test engineering	no. of engineering change revisions	20	18	15	53	126,000	Eng	283,000
7 Distribution	% traced directly to customers	30	30	40	100	437,500	Sales/Dist	
8 Sales & marketing expenses	% of sales revenue	36	38	26	100	81,000	Sales/Dist	
9 Invoicing	no. of invoices	25	30	25	80	35,000	Sales/Dist	553,500
10 Materials management	no. of stock transactions	85	65	85	235	118,000	Adm	
11 Procurement	% of direct material	44	28	28	100	130,000	Adm	
12 Order processing	no. of orders	20	35	90	145	95,000	Adm	
13 Customer administration	no. of customers	8	10	15	33	65,000	Adm	
14 Information systems support	no. of desktop units	56	32	29	117	39,000	Adm	
15 General administration	no. of direct labour hours	20,000	22,500	15,000	57,500	205,000	Adm	652,000
Total general overhead						2,251,500		2,251,500

Case 17
Smith Specialist Car Components
Noel Hyndman, Queen's University Belfast

The Company and its Products

Located in an industrial estate on the edge of Ballymena, the city of the seven towers, Smith Specialist Car Components Limited (Smith) was established 30 years ago by Kevin Smith. For the past 20 years, Kevin's son Tony, a commerce graduate from Trinity College Dublin, has assumed the position of managing director with Kevin bowing out of the management team. Originally the company produced specialist brake discs for high performing sports cars and initially became a leading supplier in the UK and Ireland in this niche market. Since then, as demand has increased, and overseas markets have opened, the company has diversified into the production of cam shaft kits and, latterly, catalytic converters for the sports car market. This has required substantial expansion and investment in expensive, largely automated production processes, particularly with the recent addition of catalytic converters to the company's product range. At the same time competition has increased, chiefly from overseas producers, and margins have been somewhat squeezed. Within Smith, there are three major producing divisions (bake discs, cam shaft kits and catalytic converters) relating to the three product markets that the company services. Company reporting to board level is largely based on product profitability statements (on a total and per unit basis). These are produced quarterly and are reviewed at board level at each of the company's board meetings.

Smith is regarded as a high-quality producer and its products have achieved particular brand recognition. Consequently, the company has been able to achieve premium prices for its products in the sports car market. Its pricing policy has been to set prices so that the company achieves a 40% gross margin on selling price. This should allow adequate margin to cover all selling, distribution and administration overheads and provide an adequate net margin. Given that its products are aimed exclusively at the sports car market, the company uses a single price within each of the three product markets and this is viewed by management as being appropriate given the similar production demands of each product within these groupings. In addition, it simplifies marketing and invoicing. Each of the product groupings use production processes common to all products as well as some specialised facilities that are unique to each individual product. The three product groupings (and their individual specialised facilities) are as follows:

Brake discs

The specialised brake disc facility consists of a modern ferrous foundry, medium frequency electrical melting furnaces, electrical autopour furnaces with laser pour systems, cold box core making machines, an intensive batch sand mixer, shakeout drums, shotblasters and automated fettling machines. The company has adopted a new process control system to control and secure production quality. Full process control is maintained with innovative measuring systems throughout the process. While the brake disc manufacturing facility is fairly mechanised, it is a relatively simple production process which significantly relies on highly skilled operators. Indeed, over 70% of Smith's production staff are employed in this facility. It is anticipated that sales of brake discs for the current year will be €24 million.

Cam shaft kits

Cam shaft production at Smith commenced 15 years ago. The specialised cam shaft facility consists of three four-axis lathes which work on bought-in and in-house produced aluminium castings and machined components. An electric servo motor is used to vary the valve timings required to very precise levels of accuracy. Sequential automatic hydraulic clamping and unclamping processes are used and changes to the machines are facilitated by the use of sophisticated linked software. Quality inspections take place throughout the process with a final inspection being carried out using a dedicated 44-channel measuring station that tests critical dimensions. Budgeted cam shaft kit sales for the year are €10 million.

Catalytic converters

Catalytic converter production was seen as a way of expanding into the very high price end of the component market and, given failure rates on original equipment fitted to new vehicles, provided the potential for significant sales volume in the long term, particularly in replacement parts. This specialised facility, the most recent and most modern in Smith, was set up only two years ago and uses technologically advanced catalytic converter spinning equipment. The sophisticated production process requires no cutting or welding as the product is formed during the spinning cycle. While most catalytic converter production has traditionally been achieved by the welding together of separate half-shell sections, the flow-forming technology used by the company enables the outer part of the converter to be manufactured from a single metal tube, with the exhaust component held static on a spinning machine. A monolith ceramic brick (dressed in a flexible and protective cotton vest) is then inserted via a stuffing machine and the other end of the converter is also spun down to size. Overall, this process is extremely automated, requires many machine set-ups and individual parts/materials, and quality inspections take place throughout the process. The very expensive and sensitive direct material used requires very careful handling. Sales of catalytic converters have grown substantially over the last two years and are budgeted to reach €6 million this year. Significant future growth is anticipated as Smith enhances its presence and reputation in the catalytic converter market relating to sports cars.

Product Profitability

It is early-July and Tony Smith, the managing director of Smith, is studying the product profitability statements for the first six months of the year aboard his boat (the *Little Emily*) in preparation for the following week's board meeting. As he sails up the beautiful Lough Swilly, past Rathmullan and Buncrana, Tony views the figures and is concerned that the company is losing margin in one of its key market segments (brake discs), even though he knows it has reduced prices in this segment well below its normal selling price. He is particularly concerned about what is going on in the market and whether the pricing policy that Smith is following is appropriate. By the time he ties up the *Little Emily* near Dunree Head, he decides to text both Mae Brown (the chief accountant at Smith) and Leonard Jones (the sales director) outlining his concerns and alerting them to the fact that he wishes the item to be discussed at the forthcoming board meeting.

Some detail (at product level) from the product profitability statements that Tony Smith has studied is reproduced in Appendix 1. The company is not experiencing any significant cost variances. Previous discussions at board level have noted that there has been considerable price pressure in the brake disc market, with a range of Chinese discs being available at lower prices than Smith's target selling price. Leonard Jones decided that prices would have to be lowered to match the competition and maintain market share. This action is reflected in Appendix 1. The situation in the catalytic converter market is the reverse of what is happening in the brake disc market. Leonard Jones had noted that the prices of competing catalytic converters were considerably higher than Smith's target prices and very early in the year decided to raise prices by over 20%. Amazingly, even with this price increase, sales of catalytic converters have been well above budget. Tony Smith ponders on these issues and wonders whether it is time to change the production and sales focus of Smith; perhaps even exiting the brake disc market.

As the sun sets over Portsalon, he reflects on a recent conversation he had with Mae Brown, the chief accountant at Smith. She highlighted that the present cost allocation system in the company tracks direct costs (direct material and direct labour) to products, and then allocates production overhead to products based on a direct labour hour basis. This was the system first developed 30 years ago when the company was established (at a time when production was more labour intensive and direct labour was the dominant cost), and as new products have been added the company has continued to use such a system (more detailed information regarding the calculation of the overhead absorption rate for the current year is provided in Appendix 2. Mae had queried whether, given the expansion of the company into other markets and the significant variation in the nature of production in producing for each market, the existing costing system is giving appropriate profitability signals. Indeed, she has also questioned the wisdom of establishing prices on a cost-plus basis when the cost information may be problematical. Some months ago she had suggested investigating the possibility of developing an activity-based costing (ABC) system and had provided some rough early workings, using the production overhead budget and the production volume budget for the current year, on tracking costs to appropriate cost pools and developing suitable cost drivers. A summary of these are produced in Appendix 3. After receiving a note from Mae regarding this, and on being informed that the switch to ABC may be disruptive and costly, Tony Smith decided to take no further action. He now wonders whether he was right.

Possible New Product

Another issue that has come to the fore at recent board meetings, and one that is again on the agenda for the forthcoming meeting, is the possibility of expanding the product range by producing oil pumps for the sports car market. It is anticipated that the direct costs of producing an oil pump for high performing sports cars would be approximately €70 per unit for material and €60 per unit for labour (4 hours at €15). In a previous conversation, Leonard Jones, on the basis of his experience with catalytic converters, had suggested that Smith attempts to establish a likely competitive price as a basis for making a decision regarding entry to this market and, off-the-cuff, thought that the market would take a price of €450 per unit. On being told by Tony Smith of Leonard's views, Mae Brown commented that this approach is akin to target costing and, given her already expressed concerns as to costing, pricing and evaluating profitability of products, is supportive of such a method in this one-off case. However, she expressed concerns as to the present underlying costing system as the foundation for such an approach.

Replacement of Machinery

The subject of the replacement of machinery has also exercised management's mind recently. Smith has a general policy of keeping its machine base up-to-date as a support to the objective of being a leading-edge technology company, as well as assisting in the pursuit of efficiency. A group of machines (in workstation AA13) were replaced only two years ago. At the time, the individual machines were state-of-the-art and their acquisition offered significant commercial advantages to Smith. All of the products pass through this workstation. It has now transpired that major new innovations in this technology have been developed that could significantly reduce the running costs of this machinery. This has largely been achieved through investment by machine producers in technology to support energy efficient production methods; a move encouraged by government through the provision of tax breaks in response to major increases in worldwide energy prices. Smith has the option of replacing the individual machines in workstation AA13 (machines AA/1, AA/2, AA/3 and AA/4) with equivalent energy efficient machines (option 1), or replacing all the current machines with a single flexible multipurpose machine (option 2). Details relating to the machines in workstation AA13 and their possible replacements are provided in

Appendix 4. The cost of capital within Smith, which is used to evaluate all new investments, is 8% in real terms.

Involvement of Consultant with These Issues

As darkness falls over the Inishowen peninsular, and Tony is tucked up in his berth in the *Little Emily*, he mulls over these three key issues, all of which will be discussed at the impending meeting: product profitability; adding oil pumps to the product range; and the replacement of workstation AA13 machinery. Given that Tony Smith wants to be as prepared as possible for the important discussions that will take place, as he drifts off to sleep he decides that he will ask Noel Davidson, an independent consultant and good friend, to look at these matters.

Required

As Noel Davidson, draft a report to Tony Smith in order to provide him with some perspective on the above issues. To help you in this matter he has provided all the material that forms part of this case study. Tony Smith requests that your report should include:

1. With respect to the product profitability report:

(a) A calculation, utilising the information contained in Appendices 1, 2 and 3, of the costs of the three products emanating from an ABC system (using Mae Brown's early ABC workings information).

(14 marks)

(b) An explanation of the reasons for any significant differences in product costs that arise between the current costing system and the ABC system.

(8 marks)

(c) Any outline suggestions as to how Mae Brown's approach to ABC might be improved if an ABC system were to be adopted by the company (no calculations are required).

(5 marks)

(d) On the basis of your analysis, comments on the product profitability report and its strategic significance (he would particularly welcome observations relating to product pricing and product emphasis).

(20 marks)

2. Issues to be considered by Smith in a decision on whether or not the present costing system should be changed to one utilising ABC.

(10 marks)

3. With respect to the possible use of target costing:

   (a) A calculation of the target cost of an oil pump utilising Smith's present costing system.

   (4 marks)

   (b) A brief commentary on why Mae Brown may have concerns regarding this calculation.

   (4 marks)

   (c) Some views on the advantages of target costing compared to the existing costing and pricing system as a basis for informing pricing and production decisions.

   (8 marks)

4. An evaluation (based on quantitative and qualitative factors) of the possibility of replacing the machines in workstation AA13.

   (27 marks)

   Total 100 marks

Appendix 1
Abstract from Product Profitability Analysis

Actual and Standard Margins Per Unit/Sales Volume Variances – Six Months January to June

	Brake Discs	Cam Shaft Kits	Catalytic Converters
Standard unit cost:			
Direct material	€27	€33	€510
Direct labour	€75	€45	€30
Overhead (€30 per direct labour hour)	€150	€90	€60
	€252	**€168**	**€600**
Budgeted selling price	€420	€280	€1,000
Budgeted margin %	40%	40%	40%
Year to date:			
Actual selling price	€380	€286	€1,200
Actual margin %*	34%	41%	50%
Sales volume variance as % of budgeted sales	5% A	1% A	25% F

*Actual margin is actual selling price minus standard cost.

Appendix 2
Overhead Absorption Rate for Current Year

	Brake Discs	Cam Shaft Kits	Catalytic Converters	Total
Budgeted production and sales in units	57,143	35,714	6,000	
Direct labour hours per unit	5	3	2	
Total direct labour hours	285,715	107,142	12,000	404,857

Production Overhead:

Supervision of direct labour	€900,000
Other labour related overhead	€738,816
Machine depreciation	€2,400,000
Machine running costs	€700,000
Engineering set-up costs	€1,640,000
Quality inspection costs	€1,566,894
Material receipt and handling costs	€4,200,000
Total	**€12,145,710**

Overhead absorption rate = $\dfrac{€12,145,710}{404,857}$

= €30 per direct labour hour

Appendix 3
Summary of Chief Accountant's Early ABC Workings

Cost pools and cost drivers:

Cost pool:	Cost driver:
Supervision of direct labour	Number of direct labour hours
Other labour related overhead	Number of direct labour hours
Machine depreciation	Number of machine hours
Machine running costs	Number of machine hours
Engineering set-up costs	Number of machine set-ups
Quality inpection costs	Number of quality inspections
Material receipt and handling costs	Value of material used and purchased

Total consumption of each cost driver by each product:

	Brake Discs	Cam Shaft Kits	Catalytic Converters
Direct labour hours	285,715	107,142	12,000
Machine hours	114,286	107,142	60,000
Number of machine set-ups	200	200	500
Number of quality inspections	100	150	300
Value of direct material used	€1,542,861	€1,178,562	€3,060,000

Case 18
Halvey's Bakery
John Doran and Margaret Healy, University College Cork

Overview of the Company

Halvey's Bakery was established in Macroom over twenty years ago by Annie and Denis Halvey as a small, family-run enterprise whose main objective was to supplement the Halvey family income. About 15 years ago, Halvey's survived the bitter bread-based price wars fought by the multiples in the Irish marketplace. This period saw the departure of many of the old established companies at the time, with only the very strongest surviving. Annie puts the continued existence of the business during this period down to their simple outlook, attention to detail and an overriding focus on product quality and value:

> 'Our motto is simple: *Putting bread on the table*. This works on all levels – it describes exactly what the customer wants – but also includes our initial motivation for starting up the business …. As long as we all remember that – good times always follow bad – then we'll keep our feet firmly on the ground.'

Recent prosperity in Ireland has led consumers to seek out greater choice in all products. This expansion in the market place has enabled Halvey's to grow its business, opening retail outlets across the Munster region, and justified the recent move to a large, newly built baking facility on the outskirts of Cork city. This move was financed mainly through existing resources within the company and did not necessitate the sale of the original bakehouse. Annie and Denis Halvey are now considering what to do with this property.

The Macroom Bakehouse

The original bakehouse is located in what was once a derelict area of town in Macroom. Urban renewal schemes and an expanding population base have however brought about rapid changes such that the site has now become extremely valuable as a potential location for redevelopment as a residential apartment block. For the time being, Noleen Halvey has taken over the premises as a location for producing a range of speciality breads. The image of the bakehouse, as home to an expanding range of speciality breads and part of the West Cork region's growing population of craft industries, is one which Noleen is keen to exploit.

Speciality Bread Production

Noleen, the second child and eldest daughter of the Halvey family, is a trained chef. She is the well-known 'face' of Halvey's Bakehouse through her regular weekly 'meal of the week' slot on national television. She also writes a daily food column in one of the major national newspapers. Her popularity is such that she is regularly asked to endorse new product offerings from a range of industries and suppliers.

Noleen has become increasingly certain that the future of the bakery lies in producing a range of speciality breads. She has been engaged in informal discussions with the management of a major supermarket chain which is interested in a rolling contract for the supply of three such breads in the annual quantities outlined in Appendix 1. Noleen understands that the supermarket group has identified a widening in their bread range as being a key input to their repositioning against key demographics in the consumer market. The supermarket merchandising manager views the Halvey proposal as offering an integrated package that would complement existing product offerings, thus allowing the supermarket chain to offer a bread range equal to, or surpassing, their nearest competitor.

Noleen described the opportunity to her parents in the following terms: 'It will offer huge exposure and access to volume business like we've never known before. Dad has worked hard to position the Halvey brand as the housewife's choice of better bread. To date, Halvey's has retained much of the costs of selling the product through its own retail chain. The opportunities of doing business with the multiples will also remove much of this expense from the P&L account.'

Annie however is not so sure of the potential of this proposal for Halvey's: 'Going the multiples route is madness. This development may compromise that market position of our existing chain of retail bakeries. Noleen simply does not realise that retail sales consist of breads for normal folk – repositioning in the market place as a so-called 'speciality' product may just turn people away – it makes the product sound too expensive.'

Given her mother's concern as to cost implications of the proposal, Noleen persuaded her younger brother John (currently training as a chartered accountant) to undertake an activity-based costing exercise to estimate the costs of serving the proposed contract. Based on available capacity and current work practices, the operating processes were summarised into a number of cost pools as follows (more detailed information available in Appendix 2):

Process/Cost	Pool Driver
Set-up (including gathering ingredients)	Number of production runs
Mixing	Weight of materials
Shaping and proofing	Number of loaves
Baking	Time required
Packing and delivery	Number of sales orders

There has been some disagreement as to the value to the bakery of the exercise that estimated the pooled costs associated with each activity. It is acknowledged by Noleen (who initiated the exercise) that the budgeted information cannot be treated as definitive. In defence of the estimates she stated: 'We have to start somewhere if we are going to launch new product offerings.' John however has contended that such exercises are artificial and a distraction from the main work of the bakery.

The Option to Outsource

To the disappointment of Noleen, John has further suggested that if the specialty bread initiative goes ahead then it should be accompanied by an initiative for outsourcing production completely. He has cited anecdotal evidence of interest in taking on such work by a former competitor of similar size which was taken over by an Irish publicly quoted and globally diversified firm in the food industry. Given that the parent company has little or no expertise in the baking industry and that its newly-acquired local branch has core competences in the cakes and sweet-dough side of the business, John suggests that this deal may be of benefit to all parties. At a recent family meeting he stated: 'Outsourcing production could be the solution to all our problems. Do we want to use the Halvey name to spend our days simply making bread – or should we now become more adventurous and let that established reputation allow us to start making money (the real dough!) instead?'

Annie is also in favour of this option, pointing out that she and Denis no longer have the stamina for long days spent managing operating activities. She is also worried that Noleen's growing profile as a celebrity chef and critic will mean increasing amounts of time spent away from the speciality bread business.

Required

Annie and Denis Halvey are unsure as to the correct course of action to take in resolving an increasingly fractious situation between Noleen and John. They have approached you, as an independent consultant, to write a report that will help them in their deliberations. In particular, your report should:

1. With regard to the proposal to expand the range of speciality breads, provide a calculation of the budgeted production cost per loaf of each of the three main lines of bread under both the proposed activity-based costing basis and under the absorption basis currently used by the firm.

    (30 marks)

2. Comment on the outcome of the costing exercise and its implications for the commercial viability of the proposed initiative into speciality breads, providing any other calculations you consider necessary. Outline the business options that may be open to the bakery to deal with the issues arising.

    (20 marks)

3. In the light of disagreement within the firm on the cost effectiveness of using more resources in the area of product cost analysis, outline the options open to the firm in cost accounting and the relative merits of each option.

(25 marks)

4. With regard to the outsourcing option, comment on the risks and benefits arising on the suggested outsourcing of production.

(25 marks)

Total 100 marks

Appendix 1
Specialty Breads – Estimates of Costing and Production Information

	Harvest Pan	Sultana Loaf	Bagel Loaf
Projected units of output (loaves)	8,000,000	600,000	4,000,000
Production batch size (average)	100	15	50
Sales order batch size (average)	50	15	50
Direct material cost – per loaf	€0.05	€0.09	€0.06
Direct labour cost – per loaf	€0.03	€0.04	€0.03
Weight of materials – grams per loaf	400	450	300
Baking time required – minutes per batch	40	50	25
Proposed selling prices – per loaf	€0.20	€0.30	€0.25

Appendix 2
Expected Overhead Costs

The expected overhead costs associated with the level of activities described in Appendix 1 are as shown below.

Cost Pool	Cost Driver	Budgeted Cost (€)
Set-up (inc. gathering ingredients)	No. of production runs	440,000
Mixing	Weight of materials	122,000
Shaping and proofing	Number of loaves	80,000
Baking	Time required	255,000
Packing and delivery	No. of sales orders	150,000

Case 19
Chicken Pieces
Peter Clarke, University College Dublin

Background

Jim Hanlon and Ray Fullam renewed acquaintances at a Christmas party of their former employer. Both had become good friends while studying and playing rugby on the 3rd Bs at College. Both accepted the job offer, on graduation, from Bates and Co., Chartered Accountants – after an endless round of tedious presentations by, and interviews with, the various Accountancy firms.

Jim took up the position as a trainee accountant and Ray entered the management consultancy and business services division. After a few years, their careers took different paths and they lost contact with each other. Jim qualified as a chartered accountant and now owned a small accountancy practice on the outskirts of Dublin. Ray continued with his management consultancy career. Now, they had met again after five years and Ray was the more worried of the two. After a while, he explained to Jim that he has 'business problems.' Eventually, Ray explained his current situation.

Overview of the Company

At the start of the year Ray had been appointed as managing director of Chicken Pieces, a company that manufactured ready-made chicken foods for consumers in Ireland. Cooking and eating habits of Irish people have been transformed during the past decade. For example, it is estimated that Irish people only spend one-sixth of the time on cooking meals compared with a few decades ago. This is a reflection on busy lifestyles and also on the fact that, with ready-to-cook foods available, there is generally less waste that requires disposal. Noting this trend towards convenience foods, the company began to produce packaged, ready-to-cook chicken pieces some years ago.

As a food, chicken is now more popular then ever to eat, even though demand has been recently curtailed as a result of people's fear about the bird-flu virus. Chicken is widely available, economical, and, because it is relatively low in fat and a good source of protein, is increasingly appreciated for its contribution to a healthy diet. Chicken is also incredibly versatile since it lends itself to many different recipes and styles of cuisine – as any recipe book will demonstrate. Thus, modern consumers are prepared to pay a premium for the convenience of ready-to-cook meals.

Ray explained: 'I took over the business last January and I hired a part-time bookkeeper to keep all the records straight but he resigned a few days ago. I don't think he was very comfortable in the job. There is no management accounting system in place and I'd really appreciate some professional help, if you could afford the time.'

Some days later Jim Hanlon arrived at the premises of Chicken Pieces. Jim's first impression of the plant and its surroundings was not very favourable but he managed to hide his feelings as he shook hands with Ray Fullam and exchanged New Year's greetings. After the usual pleasantries, Ray outlined his business operations.

Current Operations

'At the moment we focus only on the convenience and ready-to-cook consumer market in chicken pieces. We have three major products namely, breasts, wings and legs. Next year we would like to expand our product range.'

'Can you give me an overview of your operations?' asked Jim.

'Well, that's easy,' responded Ray. 'There are a few different processes involved' and as he spoke he drew a rough diagram on a piece of paper (Appendix 1).

He continued: 'We have one major supplier who provides us with all our chickens. When the carcasses are delivered they are immediately put into cold storage and they are eventually inspected for quality. Subsequently, the carcass is taken out of storage, washed and cleaned and sent for jointing. This jointing process involves cutting through the elastic tendons and cartilage that surround the joint, rather than cutting through solid bone. This operation is highly labour intensive but involves little expensive equipment other than a good, sharp boning knife and a dishwasher-safe acrylic cutting board. The jointing operation ends when the different products first emerge, namely, breasts, wings and legs. From each chicken we get two breasts, two wings and two legs. The leftovers are considered as waste and disposed of.'

'The breasts are then transferred to a filleting process. Initially, deboning of the breasts cuts away the breastbone and ribs. Removing the bones from chicken parts makes them cook faster. Tendons are also cut away. Once everything is done, the product is sealed in a cellophane wrapper and is ready for distribution. None of our finished product is held in stock. The wings and legs undergo a similar but separate process and, in order to prevent confusion, we call this the finishing process. However, this work applies only to the wings and legs. Basically, excess parts, including fat are trimmed away. When completed the products are wrapped in cellophane and cardboard, dated and stamped and are ready for distribution. Again, we hold no stock of finished goods.'

'Who are your main customers?' asked Jim.

'Well, at the moment we have only three customers: Buns, Mossgo and Superdim. We produce under their brand so we don't sell anything under our own name.'

'So, what's the problem?' quizzed Jim.
'Actually, the immediate problem is a shortage of good operating and financial data, so it's difficult to say where the problem lies.'

Ray Fullam continued: 'At the start of the year I signed contracts with our three customers to supply them with their own brand of chicken pieces for one year. They were difficult to deal with and the only way that you could get them to sign a contract was to pay a type of 'Hello' money. This required me to take out extensive advertising space in their outlets. Then, they require special delivery dates. In order to comply with their delivery requirements we do all deliveries by special courier – that's why our distribution costs are so high. If you don't do what they want, they won't pay you for months!'

'Basically, I think the business has great potential. The concept of ready-to-cook chicken pieces is firmly established with consumers of all ages. However, we need to take a close look at our day-to-day operations since all the contracts with our customers are up for renewal. I suspect that we may be under competitive pressures, so I need accurate cost information.'

'However, one advantage for us is that food sold in supermarkets in Ireland must indicate the country of origin on the label. Therefore, being an Irish producer gives us a bit of an edge since our produce must conform to EU food regulations. Did you know that such labelling is not required for restaurants? So, that if you ask for, say, Thai chicken when you eat out in Dublin, the odds are that you are, literally, eating Thai chicken! In fact, Ireland imports about 50,000 tonnes of chicken each year because, for example, Asian chickens can be purchased at about 40% less than EU-produced chicken. Obviously, production costs in Asia are much lower than in the EU as production is carried on at density levels which would be unacceptable in Europe. Also, some chickens fillets imported into Ireland had been found to contain cattle and pig proteins! For example, the Food Safety Authority of Ireland (FSAI) once discovered animal DNA in some imported chicken fillets. The investigation also found that fillets were being 'bulked up' with water to make them look bigger. Some contained just 55% meat.'

The Assignment

He continued: 'The periodic accounting reports that I receive are useless and I could never find out what was my unit cost but I was told that its calculation was too complicated! I don't see what the problem is, as I consider that the only real variable cost we have is the purchase of chickens. All our other costs can be considered fixed, because they don't fluctuate with volume. For example, our distribution expenses are a fixed cost in the sense that sometimes we hire the courier to deliver a dozen chickens and at other times he delivers ten dozen to the same location.'

Some time later that day, Ray Fullam gave Jim some operating data for the recent year (see Appendix 2) and was rather apologetic because that was all he had. He closed the door of Jim's temporary office very quietly.

Jim was grateful for the privacy and wondered just what he had let himself in for. He remembered how dull the topic of joint and process costing had seemed to be while he was at college. He now realised the relevance and importance of such issues. Accurate product costs were urgently required to allow future contracts to be successfully negotiated and for the company to engage in modern cost management techniques.

His thoughts were disturbed by the vibration of his mobile phone. It was his wife. Since he intended to work all day, Jim enquired what was for dinner that evening. 'Chicken' was the reply and Jim declined to pursue the conversation further…

Required

You are to present a memorandum to Ray Fullam to include coverage of the following tasks:

1. Based on the limited information provided in this case study, identify four critical success factors of a non-financial nature for this business, and indicate how they should be measured?

(12 marks)

2. Apportion the 'joint costs' of the storage/jointing operation on the physical output basis. Clearly show your calculations, and briefly describe the limitations of using the physical units method for apportioning joint costs.

(18 marks)

3. Prepare, in T-account format, the separate process accounts for:
(a) The preparation of chicken breasts, i.e. filleting, and
(b) The preparation of wings/legs, i.e. finishing.

(25 marks)

4. Prepare a summarised a cost/income statement for Ray Fullam's manufacturing plant for the recent accounting period. Your statement should be in the format of:

>Sales revenue
>Cost of goods sold (breasts)
>Cost of goods sold (wings/legs)
>Non-production expenses
>= Net profit or loss for the period

(20 marks)

5. Calculate the breakeven point (in sales revenue) for the year.

(10 marks)

6. The annual cost of disposing of waste material to the company in the 'jointing' process amounts to €14,000. Recently a pet food manufacturer, who is willing to collect such waste on a monthly basis, approached the company (previously it was disposed of by the company on a weekly basis). The company is interested in, effectively, outsourcing the disposal problem to the pet food manufacturer, as he is willing to pay an annual sum of €3,000. However, Chicken Pieces will have to invest in additional storage facilities, costing €8,000 per annum. Clearly present you calculation as to whether this proposal is financially attractive to the company, and identify other factors that should be taken into consideration before a final decision is made.

(15 marks)

Total 100 marks

Appendix 1
Chicken Pieces Manufacturing Operations

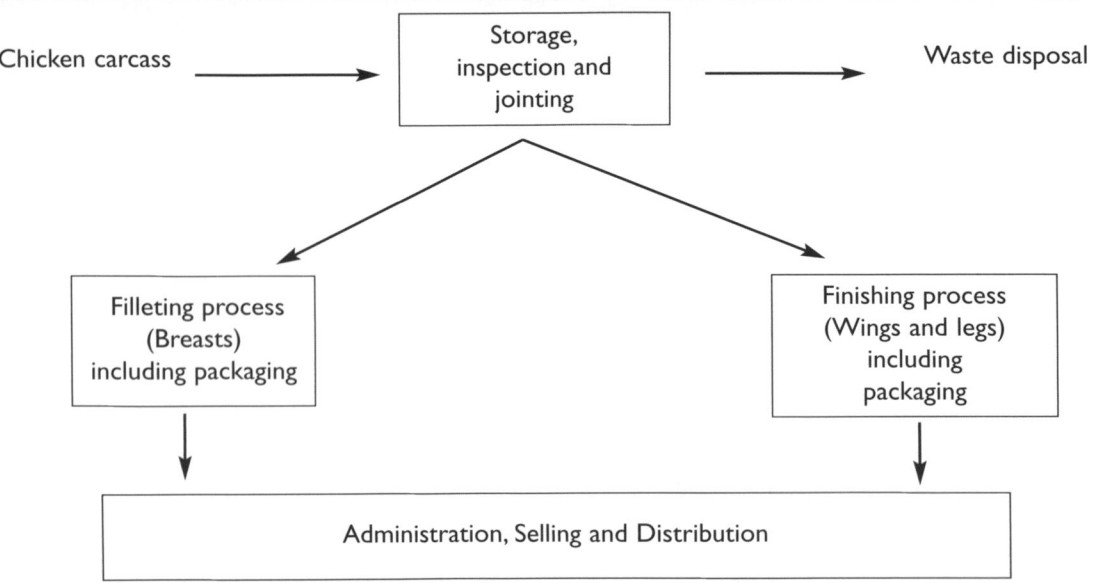

Appendix 2
Operating and Financial Data

1. Sales Data

	Buns	Mossgo	Superdim	Total
Sales – Breasts (units)	30,000	20,000	20,000	70,000
– Breasts (selling price)	€2.00	€1.90	€2.10	
– Wings and legs (units)	60,000	60,000	20,000	140,000
– Wings and legs (selling price)	0.80c	0.60c	0.90c	
– Cash received to date	€50,000	€20,000	€35,000	

2. Operating Data

Chickens purchased (carcass) and put into storage	40,000 chickens
Cost of chicken (carcass) purchased and paid for (total)	€24,000
Chickens in storage at year end (unprocessed and in storage)	5,000 chickens
Storage and other joining costs	€70,000
Waste disposal costs of jointing process	€14,000
Conversion costs of filleting process (re breasts)	€32,500
Conversion costs of finishing process (re wings/legs)	€31,000
Administrative costs	€25,000
Selling and distribution costs	€60,000

You may assume that apart from the unused chicken carcasses at the end of the year, there was no other opening or closing stock of raw materials, WIP or finished goods.

Section B

Cases in Business Finance

Case 20
The Pottery Company Limited I
Ann-Marie Ward, Queen's University Belfast

Overview of the Company and Directors

This case centres on several issues relating to the management of working capital within the Pottery Company Limited (PCL). The PCL is about sixty years old, is located in Fermanagh and manufactures, distributes and retails two designs of fine china. The products it manufactures are considered to be luxury goods, and are more ornamental than practical. All manufacturing takes place in the Fermanagh site, though the company has a distribution depot in Dublin to service its sales in the south of the country. This depot stores inventories, and distributes them on demand to department stores and gift shops in the Republic. PCL also sells some of its products to an Irish distribution company which sells the china to large department stores in various foreign countries. The company has two retail outlets; one is situated at its distribution depot in Dublin and the other at its factory in Fermanagh.

The company has four directors, with differing backgrounds. T. Brewster is the managing director. M. McGrath is the sales and marketing director. B. Owen is the credit control director and R. Gallagher is director of production.

The Principle Issues

The finance director (M. Lyttle) left the company two years ago as he and his family emigrated to Spain. The other directors have not yet replaced the finance director. The directors hold a meeting to discuss the current cash crises that the company is encountering and to determine whether a new finance director should be appointed. They decide at the end of the meeting that they should advertise for a new finance director, and recruit a candidate only if that person can deal with the issues faced by the company at present. You, a potential candidate for the post, are provided with the minutes from the directors' meeting, extracts from the financial statements for the years 2XX3 and 2XX5 (Appendix 1) and cost and revenue budget material for the growth strategy adopted by the directors on the 1st January 2XX4 (Appendix 2). The relevant parts of the minutes of the directors' meeting are as follows.

Excerpt from the Minutes of the Directors' Meeting on 14th January 2XX6:

T. Brewster (when looking at PCL's balance sheet and extracts of their income and expense information for the years ended 31st December 2XX3 and 31st December 2XX5 – Appendix 1): 'I cannot understand our current situation; PCL is a strong company. We seem to have done better since Lyttle left. He was always so negative about some of the ideas suggested and seemed to be stifling the development of the company. Yet, now that he is gone I cannot but help feel that we have maybe made some incorrect decisions.'

M. McGrath: 'I am also confused by the current situation. I do not mean to 'brag', but my team have performed brilliantly. In the past two years sales have more or less doubled. We have all worked so hard. The marketing campaign is a great success and only costs €1.5 million each year. The new sales staff have been very productive. Their salaries are only €400,000 per year.'

R. Gallagher: 'I do not think the praise should go to your team only. My team has really risen to the challenge. The shop floor staff have worked tirelessly over the past two years. Indeed, all of them have worked every Saturday. They were paid an overtime rate, but it is only for one day each week. I made sure production was not disrupted by pursuing a good inventory management policy. The purchasing manager knows to keep three months raw material clay inventory in store; I check with him on a regular basis. In addition, I do not think that you (*McGrath*) can ever say that you had to wait for a product. We make it a priority to keep the stores as full as we can.'

B. Owen: 'I have been looking into the costings. R., your staff may have worked hard, however, the Saturday overtime rates have increased the cost of wages to 63% of the average sales price of the product and this must have impacted on profitability. In addition, paying the suppliers late has also affected the price of raw materials, which have increased to 12%. I was talking to the main supplier on Thursday and he stated that he would be willing to reduce the price to the 2XX3 level, if we returned to the original payment terms. With respect to my department, I also have additional costs to report to those originally expected. We did as well as we could, given the circumstances. The increased sales did place the company at more risk. We did not get sufficient time in some instances to appropriately check the credit risk associated with some of the new customers. The result; an increase in overall bad debts from 1% to 1.5%. Though, I suppose, a half a percent increase is probably worth it given the 96% increase in sales. We have managed to keep the credit days steady at about 50 days. However, other Pottery manufacturers give 30 days credit and incur bad debts of 1%, even with internet services. My department may be able to achieve this if we could hire an additional member of staff. I expect this would cost about €36,000 per year.'

T. Brewster: 'I think when we decided to go ahead with the new marketing campaign and to increase our production we maybe did not consider the whole cost situation. I have been playing golf with a colleague who manages a successful retail factory and he says that his finance director keeps going on about the importance of working capital management and just how costly it can be to a business if an appropriate policy is not adhered to. He started to explain how types of policies are suited to different economic conditions. However, it was a quick conversation. I think he said policies could be regarded as 'aggressive, neutral or conservative.' I did not enquire any further as I did not want him to think that PCL did not have a policy in place. Remember, Lyttle kept talking about working capital and its cost. I have been thinking that this maybe has been a factor in our deteriorating liquidity position. I have pulled together our initial proposals for this expansion and noticed that we do not have any cost for working capital (see Appendix 2). Do any of you know what this cost is?'

B. Owen: 'It is something to do with the length of time debtors take to pay. I am pretty sure that credit control is a part of working capital management, but must stress that the debtor days have not changed. Therefore there should not be any additional cost in that respect.'

M. McGrath and R. Gallagher: 'We both do not think that working capital has much to do with sales or production. I mean the money comes in and goes out. It's just larger amounts, isn't it?'

T. Brewster: 'I am not so sure. I know that the purchasing manager is unhappy as he has to keep negotiating longer credit periods with suppliers because of our financial position. Anyway, I know that we all agreed that the four of us could manage the company without the assistance of a finance director; however, I am not so sure now. I think we need someone to take a look at the decisions we made again and to consider the cost of working capital. In addition, we need to get some advice on how to pull our company back into a stronger financial position. I mean, it is still profitable, though the bank is getting a little worried and is charging 15% on our overdraft. When Lyttle left he had a fixed rate agreed of 8%. The bank manager wishes to meet with us in March to discuss the future of the company. This gives us time to put corrective action in place.'

B. Owen: 'I agree. But let's not rush into this. A finance director costs a lot of money circa €100,000 per year. Is it worth it? I mean it's not as if a finance director generates sales, produces the china, or gets the money in.'

M. McGrath: 'Maybe so, but the company did have a stronger financial position when we had one.'

B. Owen and R. Gallagher: 'That is true. We do need some guidance in our decision making in respect of finance issues.'

T. Brewster: 'That is settled then; we all agree that we will recruit a finance director. Though I have been thinking they should justify their presence. So let's give the prospective candidates our initial proposal, copies of the financial statements from 2XX3 and 2XX5 and ask them to write a report evaluating the initial growth proposal.'

R. Gallagher: 'We should also get them to explain working capital to us.'

B. Owen: 'Yes, they could make suggestions on how to strengthen the company's cash position. Highlight the fact that we do not wish to lose any of our staff. Demand cannot be serviced without some overtime from our current team. R., are the machines working at full capacity?'

R. Gallagher: 'No. There is excess capacity.'

T. Brewster: 'I'm getting hungry. I will prepare packs for each candidate and ask them to write a report and prepare a presentation of their key findings. I will even include the minutes of this meeting so they are fully aware of our views. Right then, let's have lunch.'

Required

In preparation for your interview, write a report to the directors of PCL (to be forwarded to the directors with your CV by the deadline), include:
(Assume no inflation)

1. An explanation of working capital management and the different types of policy that can be pursued, suggesting which policy might be best for PCL under the current economic climate in Ireland.

    (25 marks)

2. An evaluation of the company's performance, liquidity, working capital position and how it has changed over the period 31st December 2XX3 to 31st December 2XX5. Suggest improvements for PCL's working capital management.

    (30 marks)

3. An evaluation of the growth strategy schedule (Appendix 2) adopted by the directors in 2XX4. Adjust the original schedule to take into account any changes to costs as a result of the actual working capital policy followed and any errors or omissions.

    (20 marks)

4. A re-prepared growth strategy schedule wherein a similar working capital policy to that in existence in 2XX3 is maintained. Assume that the company can change its trade receivables credit period to match that of companies in the same industry.

(20 marks)

5. In light of these workings suggest immediate measures that can be implemented to ease PCL's current liquidity problems.

(5 marks)

Total 100 marks

Appendix 1
Balance Sheet for PCL for the Years Ended 31st December 2XX5 and 2XX3

	2XX5 €'000	2XX3 €'000
Non-Current Assets		
Tangible assets	21,500	24,000
	21,500	24,000
Current assets		
Inventories	42,500	9,000
Trade receivables	39,500	20,500
Cash	-	150
	82,000	29,650
Total assets	103,500	53,650
Equity and reserves		
Share capital	1,500	1,500
Reserves	42,000	45,900
	43,500	47,400
Current liabilities		
Bank	50,000	3,750
Trade payables	10,000	1,500
	60,000	5,250
Total Equity and Liabilities	103,500	52,650

Extract Information From the Income Statements for the Years Ended 31st December 2XX5 and 2XX3.

	2XX5 €'000	2XX3 €'000
Income	294,160	150,000
Gross profit	44,124	30,000
Net income	2,941.6	7,500

Appendix 2
Initial Proposal for the Growth and Development of PCL
(Implemented on 1st January 2XX4)

Sales and Marketing Director's Contribution

Current situation (see also the information in Appendix 1)
At present we sell six million units of china each year at a weighted average sales price of €25.00. Half of the units are priced at €27.00 and are sold in Ireland. The remainder are priced at €23.00 and are purchased by the foreign distributor. Each unit costs approximately the same to manufacture. The distribution company does not take responsibility for any credit risk, claiming bad debts from future sales amounts owing from them to PCL.

New campaign
Expenditure on marketing in foreign countries is expected to increase sales to the distributor by five million units per annum. It is expected to cost €1 million. Ten additional sales staff are required at a cost of €40,000 each.

An additional sales campaign is suggested for Ireland. This involves setting up an internet sales function based in the Dublin depot. A website will be established at a cost of €50,000 each year and advertising costs should amount to €0.5 million. Four more staff are required, at a total cost of €300,000. We expect to sell 1.2 million pieces in this manner. As internet transactions are 'virtually free' we can afford to sell the products cheaper (about 10% cheaper). Though we need to be realistic, most catalogue companies give credit, and we already give 50 days credit to the retailers and the distribution company. To be attractive we should use similar terms.

Production Director's Contribution

The finance director has an agreement with the suppliers wherein they deliver the raw materials required (clay) each day before the factory opens. We pay them very quickly to secure this arrangement, quicker than we get monies in for sales. I am sure that we could take a longer credit period. I think we should keep three or four months of the clay in inventories. It would be very costly if we ran out of clay, as all the staff would have to be paid anyway. It is only 10% of the average sales value of the china (as is indirect costs), whereas wages account for 60% of the average sales value of the items. There is nothing worse than not having sufficient inventory when trying to achieve growth. We will endeavour to keep the store houses full.

Credit Control Director's Contribution

I would be a little worried about the internet sales. We do not have a system in place to deal with checking the credit worthiness of these customers. I would need another two staff to deal with the increased volume of business. I estimate that they will cost about €30,000 each. This should ensure that bad debt levels remain at 1%.

Appendix 2 (continued)

Growth Strategy: Expected Revenue and Expenditure

General Manager

The directors agreed the following expectations

	Distributor €'000	Ireland €'000
Income (5,000,000 × €23.00)	115,000	
Income (1,200,000 × €27.00)		32,400
Cost of goods sold (115,000,000 × 80%)	(92,000)	
(32,400,000 × 80%)		(25,920)
Additional Contribution before fixed costs	23,000	6,480
Advertising cost	(1,000)	(500)
Additional sales staff	(400)	
Additional internet staff		(300)
Additional credit control staff (€30,000 × 2)		(60)
Internet software costs		(50)
	21,600	5,570
Total net contribution from additional sales		27,170
Bad debts (€115,000,000 + €32,400,000) × 1%		(1,474)
Expected additional profit		25,696

Case 21
The Pottery Company Limited 2
Ann-Marie Ward, Queen's University Belfast

Overview of the Company and Directors

The Pottery Company Limited (PCL) is owned by a consortium of local individuals from Fermanagh. The company is about 60 years old, is located in Fermanagh and manufactures, distributes and retails two designs of fine china. The products it manufactures are considered to be luxury goods, and are more ornamental than practical. All manufacturing takes place in the Fermanagh site, though the company has a distribution depot in Dublin to service its sales in the south of the country. This depot stores inventories, and distributes them on demand to department stores and gift shops. PCL also sells some of its products to an Irish distribution company which sells the china to large department stores in various foreign countries. The company has two retail outlets; one is situated at its distribution depot in Dublin and the other at its factory in Fermanagh.

The company has four directors, with differing backgrounds. T. Brewster is the managing director. M. McGrath is the sales and marketing director. B. Owen is the credit control director and R. Gallagher is director of production.

Principle Issues

The finance director (M. Lyttle) left the company two years ago as he and his family emigrated to Spain. After M. Lyttle left, the company pursued a growth strategy which resulted in the company doubling its sales. However, the company is less profitable than it had been before the strategy was implemented and is having serious liquidity problems (see Appendix 1). The bank manager has stated that the bank is unwilling to extend the overdraft limit. Moreover, the bank manager has informed T. Brewster that the bank is considering withdrawing its support from the company. T. Brewster is meeting the bank manager in March to discuss the company's future. At present the bank is charging 15% on the facility. This reflects the increased credit risk that the bank is facing. In 2XX3, the rate was 8%.

Changes to Income and Costs

Sales

At present the company sells 12,200,000 units of china each year. 8,000,000 of these are to a distributor who re-sells the china in foreign countries. A special price of €23.00 is agreed with the distributor. 3,000,000 of the units are sold in Ireland for €27.00; the remainder are internet sales, which attract a 10% discount on the normal sales price of €27.00. Sales demand occurs evenly over the period. Customers currently take on average 50 days to pay their accounts and bad debts are 1.5% of gross sales. In 2XX3 the company sold 6,000,000 units of china at an average price of €25.00.

Cost of sales

Before M. Lyttle left in 2XX3, the variable costs associated with producing each unit of china was about 80% of its average sales price at the time (€25.00). However, this has crept up to 85% of this original average sales price. The cost of direct labour increased from 60% to 63% of the average sales price, as all staff worked Saturdays to achieve the increased production targets. The cost of materials increased from 10% to 12% of the average sales price as PCL started to withhold payment to the suppliers. Suppliers are now being paid approximately 103 days after they supply the clay. Indirect variable overhead costs have remained the same.

At present three months clay is held in inventory. The balance of the inventory disclosed in the balance sheet (Appendix 1) represents the finished good inventory.

Your Recommendations as the Newly Appointed Finance Director

You have been recruited, provisionally for three months as finance director. The current directors are unsure as to whether the benefits to be gained from having a finance director outweigh the salary cost (which is about €100,000). They have decided that if you can justify that a company of this size requires a finance director, then you will be hired on a permanent basis. As part of the assessment process, you were provided with the company's balance sheets for 2XX3 and 2XX5 (reproduced in Appendix 1) and given details of the growth proposal that was adopted (the principle issues are detailed above). You informed them in this report that they have been overtrading and that the company is incorrectly financed. You also stated in this report that if the directors implement your recommendations then the company's liquidity problems would be turned around in six months.

The Key Recommendations Emanating from the report are as Follows:

Sales

The directors have stipulated that they wish to maintain current sales levels. Your first recommendation is that PCL reduce the credit period allowed to 30 days in line with other pottery manufacturers. This will not affect sales levels. Based on your discussions with B. Owen, the credit control director, it is expected that this reduction will be experienced gradually over one month. You also recommend that an additional member of staff be recruited, who specialises in the recovery of bad debts. The assumption being that they can be reduced to 1%. This additional resource is estimated to cost €36,000 per year.

Cost of sales

You recommend that the level of finished goods held in inventory be reduced to the levels held at the end of 2XX3. Theoretically, production could be stopped until the surplus is cleared. However, the company wishes to continue with the current sales levels, therefore, it is important that no staff are made redundant, or forced to go on a reduced week (i.e., less than five working days). Therefore, you have recommended that production on a Saturday be stopped until sales levels fall to the required amount. At this point additional permanent production staff should be hired. This will remove the need to pay overtime rates and should reduce the variable labour cost back to 60%. There are four working weeks each month.

You recommend that PCL pays the supplier an amount to align the current credit balance to that of the original credit agreement of 2XX3 (i.e. payment within 36.5 days). The suppliers of the raw material clay have indicated that they would be willing to return in full to the terms of the original agreement. This involves them delivering each day's requirements before the factory opens. Therefore there will be no need to hold any clay in inventories (at present three months requirements are stored, amounting to €9,150,000 worth of raw material inventory). They have stipulated that they will reduce the price of the clay to the 2XX3 level.

Financing

You recommend that PCL obtains a €20 million long-term loan, payable over 15 years in equal monthly instalments. You provide a conservative estimate of the cost of this loan at 8%.

You also recommend that PCL renegotiate the overdraft interest rate back to 8%. The directors have informed you that the rise in the interest rate to 15% reflects the banks adjustment for an increase in credit risk associated with providing an overdraft facility to PCL.

Proposed Action

The directors have discussed the recommendations you suggested in your initial report on their working capital problems. The severity of the liquidity problems faced by the company, combined with the deterioration in the company's profitability, has prompted the directors to act quickly. They all agree to implement your proposed changes to the working capital cycle and request that you source long-term funding as a matter of urgency. In addition, they require you to prepare projections for a six month period from April 2XX6 to September 2XX6. These will be presented to the bank manager at the meeting in March. They have provided you with some additional information on PCL's costs and on non-regular cash outflows expected in the six month period (Appendix 2).

Required

Write a report to the directors of PCL. In this report:

1. Explain business finance and the role and benefits to be gained from recruiting a finance director.

    (20 marks)

2. Substantiate your reasoning for choosing long-term debt over long-term equity as the source of long term finance.

    (15 marks)

3. Calculate the funding that could be released from working capital were your recommendations adopted.

    (5 marks)

4. Provide a schedule detailing the expected monthly profits for the period April 2XX6 to September 2XX6. Assume that your recommendations are all capable of being implemented from 1st April 2XX6. Outline any assumptions made.

    (20 marks)

5. Present cash projections for six months (from April 2XX6 to September 2XX6). Outline any assumptions made.

    (20 marks)

6. Outline key information you consider the bank manager will wish to see in the business plan for the forthcoming meeting in which T. Brewster will request the long-term loan facility and renegotiate the overdraft arrangements.

    (15 marks)

7. Prepare five slides detailing key issues emanating from parts 1 to 5 for presentation to the directors at a briefing next week.

    (5 marks)

Total 100 marks

Appendix 1
Balance Sheet for PCL for the Years Ended 31st December 2XX5 and 2XX3

	2XX5 €'000	2XX3 €'000
Non-Current Assets		
Tangible assets	21,500	24,000
Current assets		
Inventories	42,500	9,000
Trade receivables	39,500	20,500
Cash	-	150
	82,000	29,650
Total assets	103,500	53,650
Equity and reserves		
Share capital	1,500	1,500
Reserves	42,000	45,900
	43,500	47,400
Current liabilities		
Bank	50,000	3,750
Trade payables	10,000	1,500
	60,000	5,250
Total Equity and Liabilities	103,500	52,650

Extract Information From the Income Statements for the Years Ended 31st December 2XX5 and 2XX3

	2XX5 €'000	2XX3 €'000
Income	294,160	150,000
Gross profit	44,124	30,000
Net income	2,941.6	7,500

Appendix 2
Additional Assumptions Estimated for the Six Months From April to September 2XX6

1. The direct variable overhead costs are paid for in the month they are incurred.

2. Fixed costs remain at the same level as last year and are paid for in the month incurred.

3. At present the non current assets are depreciated at an average rate of 10% per annum (reducing balance). No non-current assets were purchased or disposed of in 2XX5 and no non current assets are scheduled to be purchased or disposed of in the coming year.

4. A tax bill of €1.2 million has to be paid in September 2XX6.

5. The company usually pays a dividend of €500,000 each September.

6. The bank balance at the start of April is the same as it is on 31st December 2XX5. Interest is added to the statement at the end of each month and is calculated on the monthly closing balance at an amount equal to the yearly rate divided by 12. The bank has informed the directors of PCL that they will be willing to revert to the original interest rate if they are happy with the proposals for the company going forward.

Case 22
Waterlife plc
Evarist Stoja, Queen's University Belfast

Overview of the Company

Waterlife plc is a company involved in producing wet suits and other equipment necessary for surfing and diving. It was founded by Joe and Nick, two childhood friends very passionate about the sea. They started surfing and diving when they were 15 years old and were often frustrated that their gear was not good enough to cater for their needs. They could not surf when the weather was cold, not to even mention diving. Another problem with diving was that they really wanted to explore life in deep waters where the pressure was very high but their gear could not cope. It was obvious that companies producing the surfing/diving gear had not done much market research and hence were not fully aware of the specifications, design and flexibility required to cope with the situations encountered at sea.

Their frustration peaked when they went on a diving and surfing trip to South Africa on which they spent all their savings. They had been planning this trip for a year and were really looking forward to it but when they got there, they were very disappointed. The water was not particularly warm and water pressure was so high that their wet suits and other accessories were totally useless even though they were the best on the market. Their gear could barely cope with the temperature and pressure of the Mediterranean Sea and Cape Town and Port Elizabeth were both next to the Atlantic and Indian Oceans, notorious for their cold waters and high pressure. Their trip would have been totally wasted, had they not decided to go sightseeing.

When they got back home, they decided to do something to help all the disappointed surfers and divers, like themselves, who were out there. After persistence and help from their families, they finally managed to set up Waterlife ten years ago as a private company. Cost control and niche marketing, as well as high performance design and investment in research and development, led to good performance and increasing market share. Although Waterlife started as a small firm covering only the regional market, it has now significantly increased its market share. A few years ago, Waterlife floated on a small regional exchange. They issued one million shares with a book value of €8 each (the current market value of shares is €10). Debt was issued recently with a book value of €2 million and an interest rate of 8% per annum. The firm has also €700,000 in retained earnings (see the current balance sheet in the Appendix 1).

Current Situation

Although the market return of 12% and the risk-free rate of 4% mean that the cost of equity shouldn't be very high, this is not the case. A junior finance manager thinks that with a covariance between the market return and Waterlife share return of 150, and a market return standard deviation of ten, equity beta should be pretty high. He thought that this was the main reason why equity was such an expensive source of finance: Waterlife was recapitalising at a very high rate. He suggested that by increasing the firm's leverage, the cash flows would be discounted at a lower rate and hence the firm would be worth more (which in turn would drive its share price up). One of the directors was not convinced. He argued that increases in the leverage ratio would lead to an even higher cost of equity and hence the overall cost of capital would remain constant (he argued, invoking the famous Modigliani and Miller's proposition II). Although the junior manager was convinced that he was right, he could not make a case for his suggestion.

Nick, who recently completed an MBA at a prestigious European business school, could see the point of the junior manager's suggestion. However at that time, prospects for the economy were gloomy and he was worried about Waterlife being unable to meet the increased debt level commitments. Nick believes that these water sports products still remain expensive and hence are very sensitive to the performance of the economy. When the economy is doing well, people have more money to spend on Waterlife products and travel to exotic places. However, as soon as the first signs of recession become apparent, sales decrease significantly. For these reasons he believes it is a strongly cyclical business. Indeed, quite a few of Waterlife's competitors have now left the industry and some have even gone into liquidation.

More recently however, although the economy had not picked up completely, the demographic and social trends appeared to be in favour of their business. Research showed that in the national market there are around one million young people with this group predicted to increase by 4% per annum. It also showed that one in a hundred of them is likely to get involved in these sports and spend on average €500. However, Waterlife has not covered this market yet due to financial, production capacity and marketing constraints.

The company has adopted an innovative business model. Many companies in their industry own large amounts of fixed assets which they place as a collateral to support their high leverage ratios of 45% debt to value. Waterlife rents some of its fixed assets, has a much lower leverage ratio and invests heavily on research and development. There has been some speculation in the financial press however, that '…Waterlife management is taking it easy and they are not as efficient as they could and should be. The increase of the leverage ratio would make them more efficient…' Nick disagrees. He thinks that the low leverage ratio gives Waterlife the necessary flexibility to pursue its high growth investment strategies which it wouldn't otherwise have due to restrictive covenants that are placed on bonds. Indeed, bonds issued by firms in their industry are very restrictive.

The Future

Their research and development team has recently discovered a new material for making the wet suits that as well as insulating, would also protect the divers from high pressure. It is however expensive, and pursuing this idea would involve a large scale capital investment of €6 million. Joe and Nick are exploring ways to finance the project. Accumulated retained earnings can only finance a minor part of this project. They need to decide whether to issue bonds, equity or a combination of both. Clearly, the cost for each source is different. In numerous discussions that Nick and Joe have had with the board of directors, some of them have stressed the importance of finding the appropriate capital structure mix to minimise the weighted average cost of capital (WACC). Joe opposes this view. He thinks that share value is what matters, and focusing on WACC would be a waste of energy and time. In his view, shareholders care only about the value of their shares, rather than owning a firm with a low cost of capital. However, after Nick took the time to explain to him that under certain conditions the two things are equivalent, he got the point. If this is the case, he thought, Waterlife can borrow more short-term debt and roll it over, effectively making it a long-term source of funds. He was keen to explore this idea because he knew that the interest rate on the short-term loan Waterlife is paying at the moment is 5%, substantially lower than the 8% it pays on the ten year bonds it issued some time ago.

Nick on the other hand, thinks that the answer is not so obvious. He is sure that while borrowing more short term and rolling it over would help, it is not the answer to financing the investment they are contemplating. Joe's idea was not very original. Nick had learned about companies tempted to pursue a similar strategy which had quickly got into trouble. He thinks Waterlife has to resort to long-term financing and the main options are debt and equity. But which one? He knows that both have their advantages and disadvantages. While debt is cheaper and also provides the company with a valuable income tax shield, the interest payments are mandatory and could lead to bankruptcy. Depending on the severity of problems faced, liquidation is also possible. Further, he thinks that although the proposed new debt level would not be different from that of other firms in their industry, Waterlife simply does not have the necessary asset type to increase borrowing to that degree. Equity on the other hand is the safer option. It would, however, be significantly more expensive. To make matters worse, the market does not yet appear to be aware of the true value of the firm (and its' future potential). With the growth opportunities they have, the share price should be at least €12. Issuing shares would simply make new investors richer at the expense of old investors. This was tough. He decided to ask one of his finance graduates to help him estimate the costs and benefits of each alternative.

They computed that issuing €5.3 million of debt at 8% would indeed be cheaper. It would also provide the company with a valuable tax shield of €1.59 million which would increase the firm value. It would however entail other costs. Simulations showed that if debt commitments could not be honoured, bankruptcy costs would be €5 million. They estimated how likely bankruptcy was given the current market coverage (the result is shown in Appendix 2). Another cost was that they would exhaust their entire debt capacity, which meant that they could not go to the debt markets again. Experience had taught him that flexibility was very important in their business. It looked like equity was the only choice. However, Nick was surprised to find out that issuing equity would decrease the already depressed share price of €10 by €1.4. He thought that this could be due to the holdings dilution of the current shareholders but was not sure. The only thing he was certain about was that this was a tough choice which they could not make on their own.

Required

Nick outlined the previous issues to the board of directors and they agreed to hire you, as an independent consultant with extensive experience and technical knowledge on financing, to write a report in order to provide them with some objective views on the above and other related matters. This will help them in their decisions regarding the future. In particular, your report should include:

Question 1
A calculation of Waterlife's equity beta, cost of equity (re) and WACC. Why is the cost of equity so high? A discussion regarding the suggestion of the junior finance manager and the argument put forward from one of the directors. Who is right and under what conditions?

(15 marks)

Question 2
A discussion as to why negative prospects regarding the future of the economy have a more critical impact upon debt commitments rather than equity for Waterlife.

(10 marks)

Question 3
A discussion of the statement in the financial press regarding the low debt levels and efficiency of Waterlife. Is there any real reason for concern regarding efficiency? Is Nick right to think that the low debt levels give Waterlife the necessary flexibility that a fast growing firm must have? What other reasons might be behind the low levels of debt employed by Waterlife?

(15 marks)

Question 4

A discussion of the cost of capital minimisation and firm value maximisation objectives. Under what conditions are they equivalent for Waterlife? Support your answer with theoretical arguments.

(8 marks)

Question 5

A discussion as to why financing by retained earnings is the most preferred source of funds? Is Joe right to think that borrowing short term and rolling it over to invest in long-term fixed assets and a marketing campaign is the right strategy?

(12 marks)

Question 6

A calculation of the amount by which debt financing increases/decreases the value of Waterlife? A calculation of the value of Waterlife adopting the Trade-off Theory of capital structure. What is the implied tax rate? Are they right to assume that the tax shield equals €1.59 million and why? Does Waterlife have the necessary asset type to increase borrowing and why?

(13 marks)

Question 7

A discussion of the reasons why Nick thinks equity is safer than debt when interest payments are guaranteed but dividends are not. A discussion of the options Waterlife has to make the interest payments affordable if it decides to finance this project by debt?

(10 marks)

Question 8

A discussion on Nick's opinion that Waterlife's share price decreases as a result of dilution of the holdings of the current shareholders? What might be a better explanation for this outcome? On balance, what is your recommendation to Waterlife regarding the financing of the new project? Suggest some general points that a company should consider when thinking about changing its capital structure?

(17 marks)

Total 100 marks

Appendix 1
Balance Sheet of Waterlife plc 31 March 2XX5

Current Assets:
Cash and marketable securities	1,200,000	
Accounts receivable	800,000	
Stock	2,000,000	
Total current assets		4,000,000
Fixed assets		7,000,000
Total assets		11,000,000
Liabilities:		
Short-term loan	300,000	
Bonds payable	2,000,000	
Total liabilities		2,300,000
Shareholders' equity:		
Common stock	8,000,000	
Retained earnings	700,000	
Total equity		8,700,000
Total liabilities and equity		11,000,000

Appendix 2
Forecast of Income Statement of Waterlife plc (€,000)

	Probability	35%	35%	30%
Sales		2,000	3,800	5,500
Cost of sales		-1,000	-1,900 -	2,750
Gross profit		1,000	1,900	2,750
Expenses		-680	-1292	-1870
Earnings before interest and tax		320	608	880
Interest payable		-599	-599	-599
Tax at 30%		0	-2.7	-84.3
Earnings after tax		-279	6	197

Notes to Income Statement: Interest payable is calculated as 8% of the total amount of long-term debt plus 5% of short-term loan. Waterlife cannot carry losses forward/backward for tax purposes.

Case 23
Margin Limited
Derry Cotter, University College Cork

Introduction

As his plane circled over Dublin Airport, Michael Crimpson was wondering whether the role of finance director should come with a health warning. It was the third week, and third company, in succession where he was being drafted in as deputy. This time it was in place of John Flood, finance director of Margin Limited, who had come down with a bout of pleurisy. His absence coincided with important decisions which the managing director (MD), Margaret Drumm, believed could not be delayed until his return.

A driver in the arrivals area flashed a card with his name and in no time at all Michael Crimpson was whisked to the company headquarters on the north of the city. There, the receptionist issued a security pass and accompanied him to Margaret Drumm's office, at the end of the corridor.

> 'Come in Michael', said the MD, looking decidedly relieved to see him.
> 'John is out sick, I understand.'
> 'That's right. These things always seem to happen at the wrong time. Thanks for coming at such short notice.'
> 'It's my pleasure. Maybe you'd like to fill me in on what's been happening.'
> 'Well, we're at a bit of a crossroads really. On the one hand, Margin is looking at expanding, by investing in a new product, which would be complementary to our existing customised stationery lines. But there's also the possibility that we might be taken over.'
> 'I see. It's certainly a bad time for John to have fallen ill.'
> 'And then, there are risk issues as well. We've started to source our materials from the US. They're competitive, and the quality is really good. But John was concerned about the currency risk.'
> 'So you'd like me to report back on each of these issues.'
> 'Yes Michael and we're under a bit of pressure as you can see. We're meeting with our potential suitor next week. We need to know what's going on.'
> 'Well I'll get straight on it then. Let's schedule a meeting for the end of the week.'
> 'Perfect!'

Required

On the assumption that you are filling the role of Michael Crimpson, you are required to draft a report for your forthcoming meeting with Margaret Drumm. You should address the following issues:

1. **Proposed capital investment**
   (a) Calculate the weighted average cost of capital (WACC) of Margin Limited (see Appendix 1).

   (23 marks)

   (b) Recommend whether Margin Limited should proceed with their proposed investment in the new product (see Appendix 2).

   (28 marks)

   (c) Compute the project's payback period.

   (5 marks)

   (d) Calculate the project's post-tax accounting rate of return (ARR).

   (5 marks)

2. **Takeover bid**
   Using the information provided in Appendix 3, calculate a valuation range for the equity shares of Margin Limited.
   (Note: the valuation of Margin Limited should be computed without considering the capital investment project in 1. above).

   (24 marks)

3. **Risk**
   In respect of their most recent purchase of materials from a US supplier (see Appendix 4), outline what risk management techniques are available to Margin Limited

   (15 marks)

   Total 100 marks

Appendix 1
Capital Structure

Margin Limited, which has an accounting year end of 31st July, has the following sources of long term capital, and pays corporation tax at 12.5%, one year in arrears.

(i) Ordinary shares

Margin Limited has one million issued equity shares of €1 each. Current market value is €4. The dividend yield is 5%, and the shares will be declared ex-div one week from now. Dividends have increased by 10% per annum over the last five years.

Margin Limited also has reserves of €2 million, and a share premium account of €.8 million.

(ii) Preference shares

Margin Limited has two million issued 10% irredeemable preference shares of €1 each. Current market value is €1.50. The shares are currently trading ex-div, and a half year's dividend will be paid in two weeks time.

(iii) Debentures

Margin Limited has €3 million of 8% redeemable debentures, whose current market value, ex-interest, is 107%. New debentures would be redeemable in three years at a premium of 6% on par value.

Appendix 2
Proposed Capital Investment

Margin Limited is currently (at 1st August 2XX6) considering an investment in a new product, which is similar to Margin Limited's existing customised stationery range. The investment is expected to involve the following costs and revenues:

(i) An immediate purchase of capital equipment costing €2 million would be required. This equipment is expected to have a residual value in four years of €200,000, and will be depreciated at 25% per annum on a straight line basis. Capital allowances can be claimed at 15% per annum straight line.

(ii) Sales of the new product will be €2.5 million per annum for four years. Margin Limited earns a contribution margin of 50% on sales.

(iii) The new product would require that a new stores manager be recruited at a cost of €60,000 per annum. However, there is an 80% probability that a manager who is due to retire would be interested in taking up the position, at an annual salary of €40,000. If he retires, the company will have to make annual contributions of €15,000 to fund his pension.

(iv) The new product will require stock equal to one month's annual sales to be carried. Unit finished goods stock costs 30% of selling price. Margin Limited is currently considering the credit terms which will be offered to customers. Credit of 60 days is being considered, although an alternative of 2% 20 days, net 60 is also under examination. If a cash discount policy is implemented, it is expected that 40% of customers will avail of the discount. It is also expected that bad debts would fall from 2% to 1% of gross sales. Any working capital requirement should be assumed to arise at 1st August 2XX6.

(v) Annual interest costs of €50,000 will be incurred in financing the working capital requirements.

(vi) Annual fixed overheads relating to the new product are estimated at €100,000, and, in addition, there will be allocated annual fixed overheads of €40,000.

(vi) Research and development costs of €200,000 have been incurred, and a further €150,000 has been contracted for.

Appendix 3
Potential Takeover Bid

As Margaret Drumm has explained, there is speculation in the industry that Margin Limited will shortly become the target of a takeover bid. She is anxious to establish what value the shareholders of Margin should put on their company, and has provided the following information:

(i) Income Statement

	€'000
Profit before tax for the year ended 31st July 2XX5	700
Taxation	(100)
Profit after taxation	600

Left-Right plc is in the same industry as Margin. Its share price currently is €5. Left-Right plc has a dividend yield of 5% and a dividend cover ratio of two.

It is generally accepted that the acquisition of Margin Limited would allow the acquirer to significantly reduce its own research and development expenditure, with annual after tax savings of €300,000.

Properties, currently used by Margin Limited staff, could be let at a market rental of €100,000 per annum.

An acquiring company, through re-structuring, could achieve annual cost savings, pre-tax, of €200,000. This would involve once-off rationalisation costs of €800,000.

(ii) Balance Sheet

Margin Limited's net assets (total assets less amounts due within five years) in its balance sheet at 31st July 2XX5 amounted to €8.8 million. This includes unamortised goodwill of €1 million. Margin Limited has long-term borrowings (including preference share capital) of €5 million. The following additional information is available:

The net asset figure includes buildings of €600,000 which have a market value of €1 million.

- One of Margin Limited's principal customers defaulted in November 2XX5, after the July accounts had been finalised. The amount owing to Margin Limited at 31st July 2XX5 was €400,000. Inventory, included in the Balance Sheet at €300,000, was produced to the specific requirements of the now insolvent customer. This inventory cannot be sold to any other customer, and disposal costs will amount to €100,000.

- It was 80% probable, at 31st July 2XX5, that Margin Limited would succeed in litigation taken against a supplier. If successful, Margin stood to receive a refund of €250,000. No record of this was made in Margin's balance sheet at 31st July 2XX5. Subsequently, Margin Limited was successful, and the refund has since been received from the supplier.

Appendix 4
Foreign Exchange Risk

On 1st August 2XX6 Margin Limited purchased goods for $500,000, three months credit being received from the US supplier. Margin Limited has a bank overdraft of €1.2 million. It can borrow funds at 2% above base rate, and deposit funds at 2% below base rate.

Exchange rates

Spot rate 1st August 2XX6   €1 = $1.1311 - $1.1354

Annual base interest rates

€	$
6%	4%

Case 24
DalCais Aer plc

Antoinette Flynn and Mairead Tracey,
University of Limerick

Overview of the Company

DalCais Aer (DCA) plc is a well-established airline based in the west of Ireland, with a low fares charter to Western Europe and North America. This airline was founded twenty years ago and has grown to become one of the largest airlines serving Europe, carrying 15 million passengers per annum to 28 cities across Western Europe and North America. The airline has weathered the downturn in the industry with limited cut-backs and redundancies. The management of the airline attribute their success to its continued dedication to high quality customer service, delivered with a 'cead mile failte' welcome on a budget fare! Industry analysts have keenly noted that the company's commitment to a stable work environment for all employees is a vital ingredient to the company's year-on-year success. Indeed, according to the company's website, its employees are afforded *'the same value, respect, and caring attitude within DalCais Aer that is shown to every DalCais Aer customer.'*

However, over the last three years, DCA has experienced a squeeze on their profit margins due to increased competition from other low-fare airlines (Ryanair and SkyEurope Airlines specifically) and the switch to the low-fare business segment from more traditional airlines (for example, AerLingus). The chief executive officer (CEO), Clara Sullivan, noted that DCA share price has fallen over the past year by nearly a fifth and attributes that drop to increased competition. The board of directors has decided that the company needs to expand into Eastern Europe and the Balkans to remain competitive in this industry.

This new strategic direction would require ordering at least 24 new B737-800 aircraft from Boeing, with delivery dates of 2XX6 to 2X12. The goal is to grow the company to over 28 million passengers a year, flying to 40 cities in total, while providing a reliable and fun service for customers and employees alike! As part of this long-term course of action, the board of directors have decided initially to purchase five short-haul aircraft at a total cost of €15 million. In March 2XX6, the management team of DCA met to discuss in more depth the proposal to purchase five short-haul aircraft. There was general enthusiasm for the investment and the new aircraft were expected to generate an annual after-tax cash flow of €3 million for 15 years.

Management Team Meeting

The focus of the meeting was on how to finance the purchase. DCA had €10 million in cash and marketable securities (see Appendix1), but Declan Murphy, the chief financial officer, pointed out that the company needed at least €10 million in cash to meet normal outflow and as a contingency reserve per annum. This meant that there would be a cash deficiency of €15 million, which the firm would need to cover either by the sale of common stock or by additional borrowing. The latest debt market information indicates that the current yield on DCA debt is 5%. While admitting that the arguments were finely balanced, the CFO recommended an issue of stock as the optimal means of raising investment finance. According to Declan's calculations, this course of action should produce €10 net proceeds per new share issued. The current equity price for DCA is €15.90 a share (cum dividend) and the company has ten million shares outstanding. The CFO pointed out that the airline industry was subject to wide swings in profits and the firm should be careful to avoid the risk of excessive borrowing. He estimated that the current total debt to capital employed ratio was about 54% and that a further debt issue would raise the ratio to 57%, which is above the industry target debt ratio of 56%.

The CFO's only doubt about making a stock issue was that investors might jump to the wrong conclusion that DCA management believed the stock was overpriced. Indeed, Declan has calculated that the DCA share price (ex-dividend) is expected to fall by 10% after this share issue. Declan is concerned that this announcement might prompt an unjustified sell-off by investors, which is counter-productive in Murphy's opinion. Therefore, he recommended that the company explain carefully the reasons for the issue to the shareholders to avoid this possible outcome. Also, he suggested that, in order to increase the demand for the stock issue, the board should recommend an increase in dividend payment, bearing in mind that the current growth in dividends year on year is a steady 7.5%. According to Declan, this dividend increase would provide a tangible signal of management's confidence in the future of the company, and would buoy up the issue.

Throughout the CFO's presentation to the board, Clara Sullivan (DCA's recently appointed CEO) had a quizzical look and a permanent frown-line. Declan was unsure whether this was Clara's normal countenance or whether she was signalling her concern. Clara was an accountant by profession and had risen through the ranks quickly, on the basis of her decisiveness and strategic thinking and from that perspective Declan was wary of her. Without waiting for comments from the board, Clara immediately cut across Declan with her key concerns:

'Basically Declan, these arguments cut little ice with me,' Clara announced, 'I know that you're the expert on all this, but everything you say flies in the face of common sense. Why should we want to sell more equity when our stock has fallen over the past year? Our stock is currently offering a dividend yield of 6%, which makes DCA equity an expensive source of capital. Indeed, if I recall my professional training correctly, equity finance is usually the last resort for companies seeking investment funding, as it is the most expensive source.'

'Furthermore, in my opinion, increasing the dividend would simply make it more expensive. I really don't see the point of paying out more money to the stockholders at the same time that we are asking *them* for cash, although I think I understand where you are coming from theoretically. If we increase the dividend, we will need to increase the amount of the stock issue; so we will just be paying the higher dividend out of the shareholders' own pockets. I think that the type of shareholder attracted to DCA isn't going to appreciate that tactic. You're also ignoring the question of dilution. Our equity currently has a market value of €15.90 a share, cum dividend; it's not playing fair by our existing shareholders if we now issue stock for around €10 net proceeds per share.'

After further discussion and debate, the management meeting ended with a general agreement that the investment of €15 million was both worthwhile and strategically in line with DCA's long term goals. However, there was no agreement about the source of funding and the item was postponed until the next management meeting in a week's time. Clara closed the meeting by saying, 'Declan, I don't want to push my views on this – after all, you're the expert. We don't need to make a firm recommendation to the board until next month. In the meantime why don't you get one of your newly recruited accountants to look at the whole issue of how we should finance the deal and what return we need to earn on these planes?'

The Finance Team

Declan was disappointed with the outcome of the management team meeting but privately agreed that Clara had some valid points. Later that day in the executive lounge, Declan had the opportunity to ask Clara to recommend an alternative course of action, which she willingly did. 'How about this, Declan? My calculations show that the debt ratio is only 42%, which doesn't sound excessive to me, so borrowing to finance this investment is a reasonable course of action. Given the current yield of 5% and with a tax break on the interest on borrowing, our real cost of borrowing is 4.38%. According to my calculations, that is about 70% of our current dividend yield, an attractive comparison, wouldn't you agree? Based on your figures, we expect to earn an accounting rate of return of 20% on these new aircraft. Obviously, if we can raise money at 4.38% and then, invest it at 20%, that's a good deal in anyone's language, wouldn't you agree?'

Overnight, Declan mulled over Clara's comments but some of her figures didn't gel with his appreciation of this deal and the current gearing status of the company. For instance, his figures showed that the company's current weighted average cost of capital is approximately 9%. Declan based his calculations on an estimate of DCA's equity beta at 1.25, the prevalent market risk premium being 8% and the government gilt rate being 4%. The next day Declan called an emergency meeting of the DCA finance department.

The issues that Declan wanted his team to address included the verification of the figures already put on the table by Clara and an assessment of the impact of the various sources of finance on the cost of capital. Declan would then be in a position to recommend whether the company should proceed with the investment. He should also be in a position to identify the optimal financing strategy for DCA plc. Declan has set out the following questions to be addressed by his finance team.

Required

Question 1
Verify Clara and Declan's figures and calculations, making use of the summary financial statements in Appendix 1.

(8 Marks)

Question 2
(a) Calculate the current weighted average cost of capital before the investment, given a corporate tax rate of 12.5% for DCA.

(8 marks)

(b) Calculate the new weighted average cost of capital, assuming that DCA board of directors decides to borrow the investment funds required via a term loan with comparable terms to existing debentures. Assume that the increase in debt has no effect on the cost of equity.

(12 marks)

(c) Calculate the new weighted average cost of capital, assuming that DCA board of directors decides to issue new stock to raise the investment funds required and supposing that Declan's predictions of post-issue share price movement and expected net proceeds per share are accurate.

(12 marks)

Question 3
(a) Write a report to the CFO recommending whether DCA should opt to invest in this project and the optimal means of funding this project in order to maximise shareholder wealth. Base your judgment on the interpretation of the calculations in Questions 1 and 2 above and other information gathered from the financial statements of DCA and the case study. Comment on the appropriateness of using a company-wide weighted average cost of capital figure to assess individual investment projects.

(20 marks)

(b) As part of your report, elaborate on the significance of the following statement from the CEO, Clara Sullivan, 'Equity finance is usually the last resort for companies seeking investment funding, as it is the most expensive source', in relation to Miller and Modigliani's (1958) theory of capital structure.

(20 marks)

(c) In your report, critically discuss the different theoretical arguments that the CFO and the CEO allude to in the following statements (and incorporate this discussion into your final recommendation):

Declan recommended that, 'This dividend increase would provide a tangible signal of management's confidence in the future of the company and would buoy up the issue.'

Clara argued that, 'if we increase the dividend, we will need to increase the amount of the stock issue; so we will just be paying the higher dividend out of the shareholders' own pockets.'

(20 marks)

Total 100 marks

Appendix 1
Summary Financial Statements for DalCais Aer, 31 December 2XX5
(Figures are book values, in millions of euros)

Extract from latest Balance Sheet

	€million	€million	€million
Fixed Assets			219.00
Cash		10.00	
Other current assets		47.25	
		57.25	
Current liabilities			
Bank debt	29.00		
Other current liabilities	10.00	39.00	18.25
			237.25
Long term liabilities			
10% Debenture, due 2X10 (par €1,000)		100.00	
Equity and Reserves			
Ordinary share capital (par €12)	120.00		
Retained earnings	17.25	137.25	237.25

Extract from Profit and Loss Account

	€'m
Gross profit	57.50
Depreciation	20.00
Interest	7.50
Pre-tax profit	30.00
Tax	3.75
Net profit	26.25
Dividend	9.00

Case 25
Bradaun Limited
Ray Donnelly, University College Cork

Overview of the Company

One a rainy December morning 45 years ago, Arthur Pitt, the production director of QPS Foods, Staffordshire, received a phone call from an old friend, James Fallon, from Co. Mayo in the west of Ireland. James is the godfather of Arthur's daughter Penelope. James was visiting England on business and wished to discuss a proposal with Arthur. The two men had lunch in Uttoxeter during which they discussed Fallon's proposition. Fallon was sole owner and managing director of Bradaun Limited, a processed food manufacturer specialising in canned fish products. Its main brand is the Breaver brand of tinned salmon. James was approaching 55 years of age and wished to change his lifestyle. In short, he was looking for a partner who would look after the day-to-day operations while James himself took a less active role as chairman. Fallon offered an attractive package. Pitt went home that night and discussed the move with his wife. Since she was Irish she welcomed the move and his daughter Penelope was only two years of age so would adapt easily into the new environment. Pitt had no obstacles to taking up Fallon's offer. So, after 20 years as a senior manager in the convenience food business, Arthur Pitt decided to leave his native Staffordshire and move with his family to the west of Ireland.

Pitt never regretted the move. Bradaun proved a very successful company and grew substantially over the years. Fallon and Pitt were always conservative about borrowing and financed the expansion mainly from retained earnings. The 1980s was a decade of major change for Bradaun. Fallon died in 1980 and, since he had no family of own, he bequeathed his shares to Penelope Pitt, who had joined the company having left school. Arthur retired and Penny took over as managing director. Penny is far more aggressive than the company's previous managing directors. A major expansion was undertaken when Bradaun took over two continental companies: DFC in France and DPC in Holland. Both specialised in canning seafood with a particular emphasis on crab and shrimp. This expansion enabled Bradaun to access lucrative export markets, in France, Germany, Spain, Holland, Belgium and Italy. The expansion was financed by borrowing and additional equity capital. The new investors comprised a publicly quoted company, a private venture capital company and some well-heeled individuals. The Pitts' combined stake remained at 55%. The company was now large enough to be quoted on the stock market, but since it did not require any additional funds and Penny wished to maintain control (her father is totally under her influence), it remains a private company. However, to appease the outside investors Penny has recruited a number of non-executive directors. Some of these are associates of Penny, but most are appointees of the outside shareholders. The chairman Sir Rex Johnson, falls into the latter category. Sir Rex is a famous 'self-made' millionaire who is semi-retired. He currently spends most of his time enjoying his fortune: co-hosting a minor TV management game show; attending to two non-executive directorships in large UK-based plcs; and fulfilling his role as chairman of Bradaun. In Penny's opinion Sir Rex too narrowly focussed on the rate of return that Bradaun earns. He is often heard saying, 'the company must continue to earn a good rate of return on the capital the shareholders have invested.' Penny does not care that much for Sir Rex or the shareholders. She sees them as moneychangers, and sees her job at the company as continuing in the tradition of her father and godfather. She is therefore focussed on making the company as successful as she can make it on her own terms.

The Current Proposal

Bradaun is at a crossroads. It has continued to prosper and its profits since 1990 have enabled it to not only repay all of its borrowings but to accumulate a large cash surplus. Sir Rex has made it clear that he and the shareholders expect Penny to do something constructive with the cash surplus or pay a large dividend. They would also consider a share repurchase. Penny is not enamoured by the idea of giving what she perceives to be the company's cash to the shareholders. She personally has no immediate need of additional cash so an additional dividend is ruled out. Given the situation with fish stocks in the EU, she does not believe that there is scope for further expansion in the canned seafood industry, so has been looking further afield. She has spent all her working life in the seafood industry. The main processes involved here entail flavouring, preserving and packing ingredients. She has noticed the trend toward healthier eating and while she herself has doubts about it, reckons that many people are rather taken by the Mediterranean diet. She believes that the company could easily make the transition to fruit production, provided the project is carefully managed. She is currently considering the purchase of a small Spanish olive oil producer and the construction of a new factory in Spain. This factory will continue to produce olive oil, but it will be significantly expanded to can prunes and tomatoes. Since the project would require a major capital investment, the approval of the Bradaun board is necessary.

Penny asked Jack McBride, the company treasurer, to prepare a financial analysis that will help her make a decision and also convince the board of the viability of the project. Jack has done a discounted cash flow analysis for the project. His analysis, which is summarised in Appendix 1, finds that the project has a positive net present value (NPV). Accordingly, Jack is in favour of the proposal since it will add value to Bradaun.

Penny however has perused Jack's analysis and is somehow concerned that it will not assist her in persuading the board of the merits of the project. In particular, there are two parts of the analysis that bother her. First, she has major doubts about Jack's estimate of the cost of capital. He has estimated the cost of capital for the project to be 8%. His calculations are based on the notion that that this is the rate at which Bradaun could borrow the money from the bank for the project. Penny reckons that since Bradaun will be using little if any debt to finance the project, this is not correct. Secondly, she has done a quick calculation of the accounting rate of return (ROR) from the project. She estimates that the average annual ROR from the project to be just over 17%. She is disappointed by this, because the company is currently generating an accounting rate of return of 27%.

Before the proposal goes to the board it must be approved by Penelope. Just before she meets with Jack she gets a telephone call from Sir Rex. He needs to devote the next three months to his TV series and a holiday in the Seychelles, and wants to bring the board meeting forward by a week. Penny is not impressed: this proposal is the most important decision she has had to make since Bradaun took over the European canned food companies. She needs more time to think about it. She has had about as much of Sir Rex as she can tolerate. With Jack's analysis proving less than convincing she is not best pleased.

Having listened to Jack drone on about cash flow projections, shareholder wealth and costs of capital for half and hour Penny finally loses patience. 'I want to know the (accounting) rate of return on this project before I recommend this to the board' she barks at Jack. 'And what is this NPV stuff anyway. We never used such techniques before and have done well enough. The chairman, Sir Rex Johnson, and the other people on the board are only interested in profits. I cannot go to the board with this stuff. Is there any way we can reconcile your analysis with the profits this project will generate? I am also confused as to why you only used cash flows for the first five years of the project. What about the profits from year six onwards?'

Jack admits to Penny that though he has not presented the ROR for the project, it is much less than the average earned by the company at present. However, he argues that this is a less risky project than Bradaun's current operation. Furthermore he says 'We can borrow at 8% for it and the interest will be allowable for tax.' Penny is confused about this and says, 'My instincts tell me that this project could really be quite profitable, but how can I sell it to the Board if it will reduce the overall return on equity of the company? Also, since we have no intention of borrowing to finance this project, I don't see the relevance of the cost of borrowing to the decision' After some discussion, Jack and Penny decide that one possible way of convincing the board of the merits of the project would be to employ an outside firm of consultants to evaluate it.

Penny has approached you and asked you to consider the project. You establish the following facts. The average beta for firms in the processed food industry is 1.3. The average beta for firms in the fruit industry is 0.9. The market risk premium ($R_m - R_f$) is 5%. The risk-free rate is 6%. The average leverage in terms of the debt over equity ratio is 0.5 in both industries. Bradaun is an all-equity company and will remain so. Jack gives you a summary of his calculations (see the Appendix 1). These cash flows are in nominal terms.

Required

Answer the following questions. In each case fully explain and justify your approach.

Question 1
Address Penny's concerns about the decline in ROR and outline how the project should be evaluated, i.e. what criteria should Bradaun employ to evaluate the project?

(25 marks)

Question 2
Assess the strengths and weaknesses of Jack's approach.

(25 marks)

Question 3
Outline and explicate your own detailed analysis of the project and make a recommendation as to whether the new project is worthwhile or not. This analysis should reconcile the discounted cash flow approach of NPV with accounting profitability. (Hint: Adjust net income or ROR to compute residual income).

(25 marks)

Question 4
How sensitive is the NPV of the project to your estimate of the discount rate? Compute the internal rate of return (IRR) of the project to assist in this analysis.

(10 marks)

Question 5
Comment on the interaction between the investment and financing decisions in the context of Bradaun.

(5 marks)

Question 6
Bradaun has a surplus of cash: is this a problem?

(5 marks)

Question 7
Comment on the conflicts of interest between the shareholders and Penny.

(5 marks)

Total 100 marks

Appendix 1
Financial Analysis by Jack McBride

€'million

Time	0	1	2	3	4	5
Net Cash Flows	-1,000.00	350.00	400.00	400.00	250.00	200.00
Depreciation (1000/5)		200.00	200.00	200.00	200.00	200.00
Profit		150.00	200.00	200.00	50.00	0.00
NPV of Cash Flows @ 8%	304.42					
$(1+.08)^t$		1.08	1.17	1.26	1.36	1.47
DCF	-1,000.00	324.07	342.94	317.53	183.76	136.12
Cumulative DCF		-675.93	-332.99	-15.46	168.30	**304.42**

Jack has assumed that after year five the project will earn a rate of return that is equivalent to the cost of capital.

Case 26
Blackwater Hotel Group plc
Peter Green, University of Ulster at Jordanstown

The Blackwater Hotel Group plc, a company based in Dublin, is considering building a new luxury hotel located in the newly established dockland area in Belfast. The group currently owns six other hotels located in Blackpool, Margate, Dublin, Galway, Limerick and Cork. The hotels located in the UK have been established by setting up wholly owned subsidiary companies and it is proposed that the new hotel in Belfast will be treated the same. The cost of the construction of the hotel, including a hundred year leasehold on the land, has been estimated at €80 million, 10% of which is payable immediately, 50% in one year's time and the balance on completion in approximately two years' time. Approximately €50 million of this expenditure is eligible for capital allowances on a straight line basis at 4% per annum. Expenditure attracting capital allowances will occur at the same percentage rates as the estimated total cost of construction per year. Corporate taxes are levied at the rate of 32.75% per year, payable in the year that income arises. In addition, a working capital investment of €2 million will be required from the start of year three.

The hotel will have 320 bedrooms and 20 function rooms. For the purposes of analysis, the following data has been collated, based upon the financial performance of the hotel located in Blackpool, using an exchange rate of €1.65:£1.

On average, when a bedroom is occupied, expected occupancy is 1.5 people per night. The average charge per night is expected to be €140, which is valid whether one or more persons use the room. In addition, on average €60 per person per day is expected to be spent on food and drink and €25 per person per day on other hotel facilities. The gross profit margin on food and drink is expected to be 50%, and on other facilities, 20%.

Non-resident guests are expected to provide annual sales on food and drink of €3 million and €1 million on other facilities. The rental of the function rooms will provide a pre-tax contribution of €1 million.

Expected annual outlays are: salaries, wages and pension costs €5 million; gas, electricity, rates €1.4 million; and all other costs, excluding major refurbishments, €1 million.

Every five years the hotel would require major redecoration and refurbishment. The most recent refurbishment of the hotel located in Blackpool cost €12 million. These costs were tax allowable in the year incurred.

The group normally evaluates its hotel investments over a twenty year operating time horizon. However, the financial director considers the proposed hotel in Belfast to be of a higher risk and has suggested that a fifteen year operating time horizon should be employed. At the end of fifteen years of operation the hotel is expected to have an after tax value of €50 million, before any end-of-period refurbishment, and excluding any working capital released.

All of the above estimated revenues, costs and values are stated at current prices; that is, no consideration of inflation has been made.

The market value of the group's debt is €37.8 million and the market value of equity is €165.6 million. The debt consists of 12% debentures redeemable at par value of €100, in thirteen years time. The debt is currently priced at €114, ex-interest. The equity beta of the group's shares is 0.8 and the market return estimated to be 15% per annum. The current risk free rate of return is 7% per annum.

Although the current rate of inflation in the Republic of Ireland is 4% and the rate of inflation in the UK is 2%, an appropriate rate of inflation for the purposes of the appraisal of the investment has been estimated at 4% per year and this is expected to continue for the foreseeable future.

The company has indicated that it will require a return of 15% nominal per annum from the proposed investment. You may assume that there are 365 days in a year.

Required

In your capacity as the group's management consultant, prepare a report to advise the board of directors of Blackwater Hotel Group plc of the financial viability of the investment, in particular the occupancy rate (the percentage of rooms occupied per night, excluding the function rooms) that would need to be achieved. Relevant calculations must form part of your report as an appendix.

Your report should include a consideration of the following matters:

1. A discussion of how accurate your evaluation is likely to be and which parts of your evaluation are likely to be subject to significant error.

2. A discussion of how a formal consideration of all the risks of the proposed investment could be made

3. An analysis as to how the required rate of return has been derived, and whether this is likely to be appropriate for the appraisal of this proposal.

State clearly any assumptions that you make.
(Approximately 40% of the marks will be awarded for calculations and 60% for the recommendations and report.)

Total 100 marks

Case 27
Tannam plc
Louis Murray, University College Dublin

Following a sustained period of rapid expansion, Tannam has developed to become a listed company on the Dublin Stock Exchange. This rapid development and expansion means that it has in fact become a mini-conglomerate, with interests covering a wide range of activities, many of them relatively unrelated to each other. Initially established 25 years ago, Tannam began as a retail business, concentrating on television and audio equipment. Hugh Tannam had a well developed and long standing interest in specialised electronic equipment, and sourced a range of products that would appeal to both the retail and the rental markets. Rapid developments in the past few years mean that the business has expanded very considerably, and now covers a range of relatively unrelated activities, including the provision of services to the television and film industries, manufacturing, property development, recording and musical equipment. Most of these activities are conducted through a number of subsidiaries, which were acquired following merger, or the purchase of existing established businesses.

Because of the interests of its founder, Tannam began as a retailer of electrical and electronic equipment. It also developed a considerable presence in the rental market. Established as a limited company, it raised €4.25 million through an initial share issue. The first few years of trading were relatively uneven, however the business gradually stabilised, as new outlets were opened in a number of towns and cities in Ireland. After about ten years, they had established a considerable presence, with annual turnover in excess of €4 million, and a profit of approximately €250,000. To fund its continued development, Tannam applied for a stock market listing, and this was granted. However, trading patterns remained relatively unstable, and Tannam was not able to record continued stable profits every year. The business remained highly exposed to relatively short upturns and downturns in the electrical and electronic equipment market. Also, performance of the Irish economy remained relatively poor throughout this period. At this time, it was commonly remarked that Tannam had all the features of a high beta business, as it was excessively exposed to short-term and long-term movements in the underlying economy. In response to this, the issue of diversification came into consideration. Both senior managers and major shareholders questioned the wisdom to continuing such a high exposure to short-term economic performance.

In order to achieve the objective of reducing the dependence on a relatively volatile market sector, the directors of Tannam decided to embark on a policy of expansion and diversification into other business sectors. They therefore decided to seek the advice of a management consultancy, which strongly recommended that Tannam undertake this major change in overall strategy of the business. The consultancy identified its stock market quotation as one of the more attractive features of the overall business, and suggested that it examine the possibility of merging with other businesses that would be attracted by the possibility of a stock market quotation. This type of action could actually be viewed as a reverse takeover if the unquoted firm or firms were larger than Tannam (as control of the merged group could pass to the owners or shareholders of the firms that were acquired). Although such a strategic move would have implications for the control of Tannam, the major shareholders decided that this was preferable to the high levels of uncertainty associated with their continued exposure to a single industry sector. A strategic decision was therefore made to seek unlisted firms as potential acquisition targets, the ideal partner being firms in an industry sector that is not related to electrical and electronic equipment.

Three separate unlisted companies were identified, and discussions were initiated with the directors of each of them. In all three cases, there was a clear desire to reverse into a publicly quoted company. The main motivation for each was that it would make it considerably easier to raise further equity finance, which could be used to assist in financing further expansion and possible diversification. One firm, a Cork based property developer, Spollen Properties, had been expanding very rapidly, and had a very strong record of profitability. The directors of Spollen saw clear benefits in reversing into a publicly quoted company, such as Tannam. A second firm, CGU Distributors, was a distributor for a motor manufacturer and sold commercial vehicles in Ireland. The product range was relatively limited, so although this potentially was a major business, it remained medium sized in Ireland. Again, clear opportunities for further growth and development could be identified, if sufficient funding sources were to become available. The final firm was Fastnet Media Services, which provided specialist services to the media and entertainment industries. Although established over twenty years ago, it had recently been enjoying a growing reputation, as the Irish based media, television, and general entertainment businesses had been establishing themselves. As a result, 10 years ago, its directors also identified its potential for considerable expansion should sources of funding be successfully tapped.

Discussions with the directors of all these companies proved to be highly successful, and agreement was quickly reached. Under the terms of this agreement, Tannam was reorganised as a holding company with separate wholly owned free-standing units or divisions. Tannam plc also changed its name to Tannam Holdings on June 1st several years ago. New shares were issued in this holding company and an agreement was reached regarding the pro-rata distribution of these shares to those who were shareholders of the four firms making up the new group. The terms of this distribution largely depended on the relative sizes of the four firms, however because of its particularly strong growth record and its considerable potential, shareholders in CGU received a slightly larger allocation. With the formation of this group, a new board of directors and a new chairman were put in place. A new managing director of the group was appointed. Coming from CGU Distributors, the largest of the firms coming together to form this group, Tom Glover had a well-established reputation as a highly aggressive and successful manager, so he was offered this appointment. Since he had been a very sizable shareholder in CGU, Glover also became one of the largest individual shareholders of the group, as he controlled nearly 6% of all shares. As part of this arrangement, Hugh Tannam continued to have an active involvement with the group; however his interest was limited to an involvement with Tannam, now a wholly owned subsidiary of the group which concentrated on televisions and audio equipment.

Under its new leadership, Tannam pursued two major objectives. It decided to go for rapid growth through a further series of acquisitions, and it also decided to reduce costs in an attempt to generate increased profitability. In order to achieve the objective of cost reductions, two approaches were followed. Every one of the subsidiaries was closely examined to identify possible sources of savings. Also, most major management functions for the group were brought together and centralised in one location. Although Tannam Holdings was responsible for a range of very diverse activities, senior management decided that there was a considerable potential for savings following the centralisation. Each subsidiary was also established as a strategic business unit, with its own profit centre and reasonably tight budget constraints.

Over the next few years, Tannam also made a number of acquisitions. These acquisitions ranged from several relatively small businesses, each without a market quotation, to two very sizable firms which were in the distribution, and the building supplies businesses. When considering the acquisition of quoted companies, management determined to acquire firms trading at a lower price/earnings ratio than Tannam. This decision, to concentrate only on publicly quoted companies trading on a relatively low P/E ratio, was taken by Tom Glover as he insisted that it is necessary to maintain company share price. The reason for this approach was a belief that it should ensure no dilution of earnings per share in Tannam as a result of the acquisition. However, it has proved to be controversial with the senior management of Tannam, some of whom argue that these companies may be poor performers and that they may not contribute to the long-run success of the group. However, the managing director ensured that his policy was closely followed; so that both acquisitions were of firms trading on lower P/E ratios than Tannam. A list of all the wholly owned subsidiaries currently in the Tannam Group is provided in Appendix 1.

A combination of retained earnings and new debt or equity capital was used to finance these acquisitions. As Tannam proved to be a profitable group, internally generated funds could be used to finance the purchase of a number of the smaller businesses. However, as the number of acquisitions increased, including the two publicly quoted, further outside funding was required. As a result, Tannam raised a combination of new equity and new debt finance. In these cases, the acquisition consisted of a combination of share for share exchange, and a cash payment that was financed through the new debt issues. As the cash purchase of some of the smaller acquisitions also required external financing through the issue of new debt, the capital structure of Tannam became more complex, and consisted of a combination of equity, convertible debentures, debentures loan stock and long-term bank debt. In every case, Glover and his senior management team took the decision regarding an appropriate source of finance. It largely depended on market conditions at the time and the need to maintain a healthy debt ratio for the holding group.

Throughout this period of rapid expansion the management team was able to maintain a healthy dividend policy. Annual dividends were either maintained at the previous year's level or were increased. Management was able to continue this policy as annual earnings tended to remain reasonably stable. Clearly the decision to diversify the range of activities of Tannam had been successful, as the business established a strong record of annual profitability and had a relatively low exposure to downturns in the national economy. The original strategic decision to diversify business activities across a number of sectors was clearly proving successful.

Since Tannam Holdings was established, a budgetary control system was introduced, developed, and gradually improved. Before establishment of the holding group, Tannam had employed a payback period approach to evaluate all investments above an established minimum value. All investment appraisal decisions were evaluated by payback, with a minimum cut-off period of three years being established. However, with the development of the budgetary control system, management agreed to establish an appraisal system that would allow for cost of capital and the time value of money. Both net present value (NPV) and internal rate of return (IRR) were considered, and after considerable discussion, management expressed a preference for the IRR. Their reason for this was that a percentage rate of return on investment was a more meaningful measure. However, as there had been reasonably strong support for NPV, it was agreed that both would be prepared and used as inputs to the evaluation process. However, the primary measure was to be the IRR. All successful proposals had to offer an after-tax IRR that exceeded after-tax cost of capital for the group.

On a recent sunny day, the new finance director of Tannam Holdings, Gloria Knight, was considering a number of new proposed investments. As there had been a time lag between the departure of the previous office holder and Gloria's appointment, a reasonably large list of new proposals was under consideration. Budgetary control procedures required that the finance director evaluate all proposals above a pre-determined minimum value, so these proposals were awaiting her consideration. In each case, the subsidiary companies had prepared an evaluation of projects that had emanated from them and an estimated after tax IRR had been submitted. As finance director, Knight now had to decide which proposals she would support at an upcoming meeting of the board of directors. As well as submitting a recommendation, she decided that a report would be necessary to justify the decision that she takes.

Total proposed expenditure came to €80 million. This investment would be financed in a similar manner to previous investments, through a combination of retained earnings, new debt capital, and a new issue of equity capital. A recent income statement for Tannam Holdings is presented in Appendix 2. Although the precise details of the financing had yet to be finalised, it had been agreed with the board that whatever combination is employed, it will have minimal impact on the current structure of long-term finance in Tannam. To begin the assessment, Knight decided to calculate the current weighted average cost of capital (WACC) for Tannam. As it had been agreed that assessment would be based on an after-tax IRR, she decided to prepare an estimate of the after-tax cost of capital by allowing for the deductibility of interest payments when assessing company taxes. Cost of debt was therefore calculated as the coupon rate, or interest rate, adjusted for this tax saving. Bank overdrafts were not included in this assessment, as they were considered to be short-term debt and therefore not part of the group capital structure. Also, as overdrafts tend to carry a low interest rate, Knight had a concern that their inclusion might overly reduce the cost of capital. Cost of equity capital was estimated using the capital asset pricing model (CAPM). Using an estimated return on the market equity index of 13%, a risk-free return of 6%, and an estimated beta coefficient of 1.1 for Tannam Holdings, a cost of equity of 13.7% had been estimated. Details of the full calculations for the WACC are presented in Appendix 3. Appendix 4 provides a list of the proposals that are under consideration. It largely consists of proposed investments by many of the individual subsidiaries; in addition, two proposals for the purchase of small unlisted businesses are also included.

Cost of capital calculations produce an estimated after-tax rate of 11.66%, so after allowing for error, an overall hurdle rate of 12% is implied. The implication is that all proposals offering an after tax return in excess of 12% should be approved, regardless of which subsidiary of Tannam has submitted them. Using this measure, all but one of the proposals that had been submitted to her meet the minimum requirement for investment. After some consideration, Gloria Knight was uneasy, as she was fully aware that the various subsidiaries of Tannam were engaged in very different activities and would be facing very different risk exposures. Her concern was whether it was appropriate to apply the single fixed hurdle rate across all these different activities. Perhaps the hurdle rate employed should allow for these differences in risk. For example, she was concerned that the huge proposed investment in a new head office building for Quirke Construction should be evaluated at such a low rate, considering the relatively volatile state of the construction industry. It is true that construction can experience years of steady growth; however, there is always a concern that it may not be maintained. Also, an assessment of the proposed new warehouse facility for Tress indicated that it was not economical; but considering the particularly low risk exposure for the garden equipment sector, and the potential value of this proposal to this business, Knight wondered if the benchmark hurdle rate applied was too high.

In order to develop her thinking, Knight decided to make an evaluation of the risk profile of each subsidiary company by identifying similar independent publicly quoted firms on either the Dublin or the London Stock Exchanges. In order to minimise estimation error, she found firms that matched closely, after allowing for both size and industry sector. In each case, she used publicly available sources to generate a beta estimate for each firm. Assuming that these values provide a close estimate of beta for each subsidiary in Tannam holdings, she adjusted the hurdle rates to allow for a more precise measure of market risk. Estimated market risk or beta values for each subsidiary have been included in Appendix 1. In the case of Lennox Distributors, Knight estimated that the appropriate beta value to be 0.9.

Required

Prepare a report on behalf of Gloria Knight that provides the background to the current appraisal decisions and suggests an appropriate overall approach. In particular:

1. Discuss the issue of diversification, as pursued by Tannam. Outline possible benefits and costs associated with this approach.

    (20 marks)

2. Review the policy adapted by Tannam, i.e. only to acquire companies trading on a lower P/E ratio than itself. Explain the reasoning behind this approach, and consider whether it is always appropriate. Use numerical examples to demonstrate your points.

    (25 marks)

3. Critically outline how Tannam currently deals with appraisal decisions. In your discussion, consider the issue of whether a particular source of finance used to purchase a subsidiary, or to cover the cost of a particular investment, should be used to determine the hurdle rate. Give reasons for your recommendation on a best overall approach.

    (20 marks)

4. Considering the risk profile of the individual proposed investments, discuss whether a single hurdle rate is appropriate. Using Knight's estimated beta values for the individual subsidiaries use the CAPM and WACC formulae to determine an optimal hurdle rate for each subsidiary. You can assume that the balance of debt and equity capital in each subsidiary would be similar to that of the parent firm. Conclude this section with recommendations on each of the proposed investments.

    (35 marks)

    Total 100 marks

Appendix 1
List of Subsidiaries Held in the Tannam Group, December 2XX4

Tannam Limited	$\beta=1.9$	Electrical and electronic equipment – retail and rental
Spollen Properties Limited	$\beta=2.2$	Property development
CGU Distributors Limited	$\beta=0.7$	Motor vehicle distributors
Fasnet Media Services Limited	$\beta=1.1$	Equipment for media and entertainment industries
Quirke Construction Limited	$\beta=1.8$	Building contractors and providers
Kenge Haulage Limited	$\beta=1.3$	International distribution
Tress Limited	$\beta=0.6$	Garden equipment and supplies
Cross Timber Limited	$\beta=0.8$	Furniture manufacturer
Image Consultants Limited	$\beta=1.7$	Interior design
Laheen Refrigerators	$\beta=1.0$	Refrigeration equipment for the retail trade

Appendix 2
Tannam Holdings
Consolidated Profit and Loss Account Y/E December 31st 2XX4

	(€000s)
Turnover	410,812
Cost of sales	(331,906)
Gross profit	78,906
Transportation costs	(15,815)
Administrative expenses	(25,385)
Overheads	(896)
Interest expenses	(14,398)
Profit before tax	22,412
Tax	(3,362)
Profit after tax	19,050
Dividends	(6,477)
Retained earnings	12,573

Appendix 3
Estimation of Weighted Average Cost of Capital for Tannam Holdings

	Tax Adjusted Return	Weighting	WACC
10% Debentures	8.5%	0.175	1.48%
13% Loan stock	11.05%	0.035	0.38%
9% Convertibles	7.65%	0.09	0.69%
12% Term loan	10.2%	0.14	1.43%
Equity capital	13.7%	0.56	7.67%
Weighted Average Cost of Capital			**11.66%**

Appendix 4
Investment Proposals Under Consideration by Gloria Knight

	Initial Investment €'000	IRR %	NPV €'000
Improved retail premises – Tannam	2,250	17	1,450
New electrical equipment – Tannam	5,875	15	3,500
New fleet – Kenge Haulage	10,000	16	3,800
Warehouse facility – Tress	2,500	11	-350
New office building – Image Consultants	5,000	17	2,250
Computer controlled equipment – Cross Timber	625	16	450
Land purchase – Spollen Properties	22,000	15	2,500
Expanded storage – Laheen	925	14	800
Head office building – Quirke Construction	25,000	13	1,000
Purchase of Lennox Distributors	13,175	12	2,800
Total	**87,350**		

Case 28
Calvin plc
Peter Green, University of Ulster at Jordanstown

Calvin plc, an established Belfast based company, manufactures building materials. Although the profitability of the company has been somewhat erratic, over the last three years, Calvin has not needed to use its overdraft facility of €1.0 million. During the most recent financial year (31 December 2XX5) the company has reported a sharp increase in operating profits before interest and tax, from the €25 million level in 2XX3–2XX4, to €50 million. An analysis of performance indicates that whilst gross profit margins have remained more or less constant, the profitability of the company has doubled due to volume expansion as a result of an economic boom in housing developments.

Although the company has excess manufacturing capacity, due to the nature of the company's products and the associated transportation costs between Belfast and Dublin, the company has decided not to export, even though market research has indicated that a substantial market in the Republic of Ireland exists (Appendix 1 provides data on the findings of the market research). The market research survey cost €0.25 million and this account has not yet been settled. As the company has substantial excess capacity, future investment requirements only relate to routine replacements, which are estimated to be less than €0.5 million per year over the next five years.

The company's chief executive is Mark Calvin. Mark, a chartered accountant has historically followed a rather conservative financial policy, with relatively low gearing levels. The company currently has a large cash surplus and the board of directors has called for a meeting to discuss how this should be utilised.

The directors have made two main suggestions. One is to redeem the €20 million secured loan stock which had been issued several years ago to finance a capacity increase and which is due for redemption at par in ten years time. The other is to increase the dividend payment to shareholders by the same amount. An analysis of the disposition of the current shareholders is provided in Appendix 2.

Calvin's capital structure as at 31 December 2XX4 is shown below:

	€ million
Issued share capital (25p par value)	140
Reserves	260
7% Secured loan stock 2X17	20

Corporation tax has been payable at approximately 33% and it would appear reasonable to assume that this rate will persist for the foreseeable future. The dividend paid by Calvin in 2XX3–2XX4 was 1.50 cents per share.

Industry averages with regard to dividend and borrowing levels for 2XX3–2XX4 have been collated as:

Dividend cover	2.4 times
Gearing (long-term debt/equity, calculated on book value)	45%
Interest cover	6.5 times

(Earnings before interest and tax divided by interest charges)

A more comprehensive set of comparative data for payout levels is provided in Appendix 3.

Required

In your capacity as a management consultant write a report to the board of directors, advising on the utilisation of the cash surplus.

For the purposes of this report, you may ignore differences in corporation tax between the Republic of Ireland and the United Kingdom, and answer only in relation to the information provided in the case study

State clearly any assumptions that you make.

(Approximately 40% of the marks will be awarded for calculations and 60% for the recommendations and report.)

Total 100 marks

Appendix 1
Data Supplied By Market Research Report

Projected Financial Data from Exporting (€ million)

Year	1	2	3	4	5
Sales	1.0	2.0	4.0	8.0	20.0
Variable costs					
Operating costs	0.70	1.40	2.80	5.60	14.0
Transportation costs	0.25	0.5	1.0	2.0	5.0

Transportation costs relate to the movement of finished goods from Belfast to Dublin. Initial set-up costs would largely relate to legal fees of €0.5 million, payable immediately and tax deductible against the profits for the current year just about to come to an end. Corporation tax will be payable at 33%, payable in the year in which income arises. After year five, it is estimated that performance would continue as per year five, indefinitely.

Additional Investigations

The market research team also identified an existing company manufacturing building materials located in Dublin. Following an informal approach, the cost of acquiring this company has been estimated within the range of €16m to €20m. Additional investment of €4 million in new machines and €8 million in working capital would immediately be required, resulting in forecast post-tax net cash flows (after tax relief on capital allowances from year one onwards) from the acquired company in year one of €3.0 million rising to €5.0 million in year two and subsequent years, indefinitely. Due to the introduction of a just-in-time (JIT) stock control system, it is not expected that working capital will rise for the foreseeable future.

Due to the excess capacity in Belfast, machinery could be transferred to Dublin at a transportation cost of €0.5 million to the Dublin subsidiary, payable immediately. This machinery had originally cost Calvin €5 million. Capital allowances on new machinery can be claimed at 25% on a reducing balance basis. Corporation tax will be payable at 33%, payable in the year in which income arises.

The data supplied with regard to both exporting and acquiring the existing company has been prepared on the basis that the options are independent, that is the company could opt to both export and acquire the existing company, and the financial data would remain as above. If the machinery is transferred from Belfast to Dublin however, then the manufacturing capacity in Belfast would no longer be sufficient to supply the export market. The improved manufacturing capacity in Dublin would be sufficient to service the entire Republic of Ireland market.

It may be assumed that all of the figures above have been adjusted for the likely impact of inflation and Calvin would require a return of 15% from any such investments.

Appendix 2
Equity Shareholdings
(As at 31 December 2XX5)

Mark Calvin	managing director	5%
Shirley Morrison	sales director	5%
David Stevenson	technical director	5%
Gavin Rogers	business development director	5%
Institutional investors	(90% held by pension funds)	60%
Current employees	(approximately 150 employees)	10%
Retired employees	(approximately 100 employees)	10%

Appendix 3
Descriptive Statistics on UK Payout Ratios
(2XX3/2XX4)

	Mean	Median	Mode	Standard Deviation
Full UK sample	0.56	0.44	0.5	2.23
Industrial classifications:				
Building	0.41	0.35	N/A	0.28
Chemicals	0.51	0.49	0.57	0.21
Engineering	0.51	0.45	N/A	0.33
Breweries & spirits	0.42	0.41	0.67	0.13
Food manufacturing	0.56	0.47	N/A	0.59
Distributors	0.63	0.45	0.64	1.43
Retailers	0.47	0.43	0.40	0.31
Electricals	0.54	0.47	0.59	0.41

Case 29
Xia Limited
John Cotter, University College Dublin

Overview of Company

Xia Limited is a computer software specialist based in Silicon Valley in California. It currently employs 72 staff. Its history is short but very successful: It began business when its founder and current chief financial officer (CEO), James Brown, left Microsoft less than four years ago. James Brown, who was a new products specialist for Microsoft, believed there was a new niche in what he called 'old but new' products where non-computer technology products are reinvented with software innovations and support. The first product they developed was a palm pilot (or electronic diary) that had a number of extras, including telephone; radio; MP3 player; and large memory storage. The Xia Creation™ was very successful and quickly drove a large expansion in the size and fortunes of the company. Market share and revenues also grew, especially outside of the US. It currently has the following revenue sources:

- Servicing the EU economies that have signed up to the euro (45% of their trade).
- Servicing the UK market in Sterling (25% of their trade).
- Servicing the Asian markets in Japanese yen (10% of their trade).
- Servicing the US (20% of their trade).

James Brown is very interested in developing and expanding by investing directly in Europe. His market research has suggested that continued growth in European markets is very promising, but expansion in the domestic market and Japan will be more difficult because of competing firms.

James Brown has commissioned a consultancy company, International Ideas, to analyse the relevant information for the further development of Xia Limited. John Oglewski, a specialist on country risk analysis has been given the task of developing the report for Xia Limited. There are two main issues to be addressed in the report. First is the possible expansion of Xia Limited: where to expand? In particular, International Ideas are asked to assess an expansion for Xia in Scotland and the Republic of Ireland (the two were chosen for their membership of the EU but also because James Brown felt Irish/Scottish with his father being from Ireland and his mother coming from Scotland).

John Oglewski sought clarification on the project as he felt that expanding in Silicon Valley should be assessed. The reply from Xia, in a meeting with James Brown, was that whilst the company had plans to expand domestically in the future and would remain a US company by keeping its headquarters and research and development department there, nevertheless the expansion currently being assessed should concentrate on servicing Europe (EU without UK, and UK) that would avoid the associated tariffs from US exports (Non-EU tariffs ranged from 12 to 25% for the types of goods that Xia produced and would represent a very large fixed cost to exporting to Europe.)

John Oglewski also got further clarification that he had not sought at all but felt it was relevant to the project. On meeting James Brown, it was clear to John Oglewski that James Brown had already made the decision on where to locate. James recounted John with tales of his latest trip to Ireland and the great time he had fishing on the Shannon. More importantly, James Brown also pointed out that the trip was part business, and that he had several meetings with representatives of Irish trade and development organisations, including the Industrial Development Authority (IDA), Enterprise Ireland and Forfas. The outcome of these meetings was very successful and James had made his decision to locate in Ireland. It was made very clear to John Oglewski that Ireland was the preferred location and that justifying choosing Scotland would be a very difficult and possibly fruitless task. John Oglewski felt his role was merely to give Xia an independent 'rubber stamp' of its decision to locate in Ireland.

This exuberance of James Brown was clear as he enthusiastically discussed the possibility of developing even stronger ties with Ireland. James Brown noted that Ireland offered a very attractive corporation tax rate of 10% (compared to 16% in the US) and he felt that this could be exploited further by the possibility of fully relocating production (but not research and development) in Ireland, with the parent company remaining registered in the US. This would allow Xia to benefit from access to their main markets and avoid customs etc., while allowing for profits to be reported in Ireland that would be taxed at a low rate. The net profits could then be transferred back to the holding company in California. Also, profit manipulation could be further enhanced by transfer pricing between the parent company in the US and its subsidiary in Ireland. The main concern that James Brown voiced about relocation was the potential foreign exchange exposure it would face from exporting from Ireland to the US, Japan, and the rest of Europe. James Brown was also enthusiastic about the quality of other inputs into computer software development that was present in Ireland, such as the expertise of potential employees and the overall structure of this industry in Ireland. Hence the second main issue to be addressed in the report is the potential foreign exchange exposure that would result from a full production transfer to Ireland and the continuing servicing of Xia's markets.

Cashflow Data

Details of the projected cashflows of locating in Ireland and Scotland are given in Appendix 1. The discount factor that is recommended for any analysis is 5% and is based on the current cost of capital that Xia is facing (based on US figures). The figures in Appendix 1 represent net values for any year (inflows minus outflows). Xia wants the analysis to be based on five years of expansion and it is thought that after an initial net outflow both operations will tend to be profitable thereafter. The financial support of respective governments and the potential large turnover are key drivers for the quick profitability of the expansions.

Country Specific Data

John Oglewski gathered comprehensive country specific data for the purposes of analysing the new investment. Some summary data is given in Appendix 2. The data is to be used to help make a decision whether the investment and expansion should take place, and, if so, what economy should be chosen. The macroeconomic data provides average forecasts of some leading indicators over the next few years. These provide estimates of how the economies would do given the information that is available at the time of forecast and if the current situation was to hold going forward. Rankings of the skillbase, infrastructure, profit opportunity rankings (POR), fiscal responsibility and monetary instability represent values looking back over the last ten years are subjectively measured. The corporation tax and grants and support information give an indication of the respective government's financial support for foreign direct investment. In addition, it is noted that both Ireland and Scotland are open economies that are heavily dependent on international trade.

Foreign Exchange Data

Given that there were two main issues of concern (where to invest and potential foreign exchange exposure), John Oglewski felt he needed to get foreign exchange data in terms of dollars and euros but also get data over differing time-periods.

At the moment Xia export a large proportion of their product to the EU and Asian markets. In both cases they incur exchange rate exposure (potential for exchange rate changes and for exchange rate risk). Due to this, Xia Limited has developed a system where they receive payments on a six monthly basis. This policy has worked quite well in managing exchange rate exposure, as the company is only concerned with exchange rate exposure on a semi-annual basis. John Oglewski obtains exchange rate changes for the relevant economies in dollars on a six-month basis over the last five years. The values are given in Appendix 3 for six-monthly intervals detailing movements in the euro, sterling and the yen in terms of one unit of a US dollar.

In addition, John Oglewski calculated monthly exchange rate changes in euros for its main trading partners (the values are given in Appendix 4). Here, summary statistics (minimum value, maximum value, average value and standard deviation of values) are presented for a monthly analysis of exchange rate changes in euros for the three leading world currencies and Xia's main trading areas if they were to relocate to Ireland (US, UK, Japan and rest of Europe). The time period of the statistics was from 1992-2005 inclusive, representing 14 years, and sub sample values are given for an equally spaced period before and after the introduction of the euro.

Required

You have been asked to act as an independent consultant to advise Xia Limited on the best way to deal with their potential relocation and expansion. Also you are required to advise on the foreign exchange exposure implications of moving to Ireland. A range of issues should be dealt with in your report:

Question 1
You have been asked to assess the relative merits of expanding in Scotland or in Ireland based on the projected cashflows using present value (net present value analysis). Also support your answer using ratios (e.g. profitability index). Outline the breakeven internal rate of return for both locations based on the projected cashflows.

(30 marks)

Question 2
Further illustrate your analysis by commenting on potential changing of the values relating to your answer in Q1. (e.g. discount factor). Confine your comments to the estimation of the net present value of the projected cashflows (no calculations are necessary for this question).

(10 marks)

Question 3
Repeat the analysis of determining the relative merits of expanding in Scotland and Ireland using the country specific details in Appendix 2. In particular, you should comment on the assumptions underlying these forecasts and whether you feel that any variability would affect your recommendations on where to base Xia's expansion.

(20 marks)

Question 4
Repeat the analysis of determining the relative merits of expanding in Scotland and Ireland using the US dollar exchange rate changes in Appendix 3. In particular you should comment on average exchange rate changes and deviations from the average. You should also comment on the extent to which Xia's trade would be affected by this data.

(20 marks)

Question 5
Discuss the likely direction Xia should take in terms of expanding revenues based on the foreign exchange rate changes (you should assume that each market is equally profitable on all considerations with the exception of the exchange rate data) as shown in Appendix 4.

(20 marks)

Total 100 marks

Cases in Management Accounting and Business and Finance 177

Appendix 1
Projected Cashflows for Potential Expansion of Xia Limited

Net cashflows

	Ireland	Scotland
Year 0	-1000	-1000
Year 1	+300	+500
Year 2	+200	+200
Year 3	+400	+300
Year 4	+600	+400
Year 5	+700	+400

Notes: All figures are net (inflows minus outflows) and in $ millions over a five year period. The initial investment in both economies is $1,000m. Cash outflows deal with expenses such as wages etc. Cash inflows include government grants and revenues.

Appendix 2
Country Specific Details for Xia Limited

Macroeconomic Forecasts

	Ireland	Scotland
Inflation Rates	3%	3.8%
Interest Rates	3.5%	5.0%
POR	86/100	84/100
Infrastructure	81/100	93/100
Employees	91/100	91/100
Grants and support	$22m	$6
Taxation	10%	21%
Fiscal Responsibility	96/100	97/100
Monetary stability	95/100	91/100

Notes: The Macroeconomic Forecasts are obtained from a variety of sources. For example, the economic information and forecasts are mainly obtained from OECD and IMF country reports. The grants and support information was obtained directly from individual country's industrial support bodies. Inflation, taxation, and interest rates are averages of five-year forecasts in percentage form. The profit opportunity rankings (POR), represents a subjective estimate of the level of political risk entailed in doing business in a particular economy. The rankings (the higher the more appealing) represent a proxy of the business climate to new enterprises. Infrastructure covers road network, telecommunications and other background facilities. 'Employees' measures suitability in terms of education. Grants and support are given by industrial development organisations to support new businesses. Tax is the prevailing corporation tax on offer and guaranteed for Xia for the next five years in respective countries. Fiscal responsibility is a subjective measure of fiscal policies (eg. taxation and budgets), with a higher ranking being more appealing. Monetary stability is a subjective measure of monetary policy with a higher ranking being more appealing. The uncertainty relating to whether the UK would join the Eurozone is reflected in Scotland's score.

Appendix 3
US Dollar Exchange Rate Changes Data for Xia Limited

Time-period	Euro	Sterling	Yen
1	2.3	1.8	2.8
2	3.1	1.6	3.2
3	2.1	3	4.1
4	2	2.3	2.9
5	1.9	2.1	3.4
6	2.9	1.7	4.5
7	3	2	3.5
8	3.1	3.2	3.2
9	2.7	1.2	2.9
10	4	1.8	4

Exchange rate changes (absolute values) are given for the previous five years representing six-monthly interval values. The exchange rate changes are given for each currency in terms of US dollars.

Appendix 4:
Summary Statistics of Monthly Exchange Rate Changes for Euro

	Minimum	Maximum	Average	Deviation
Full sample				
Dollar	-9.37	6.97	-0.09	2.86
Sterling	-4.52	10.69	-0.04	2.01
Yen	-11.23	7.89	-0.12	3.26
Pre-euro				
Dollar	-9.37	5.53	-0.20	2.82
Sterling	-4.52	10.69	-0.05	2.10
Yen	-11.23	7.89	-0.12	3.26
Post-euro				
Dollar	-5.62	6.97	0.01	2.92
Sterling	-3.93	6.46	-0.03	1.91
Yen	-7.24	5.68	-0.16	3.25

Values are given as monthly percentage changes. All currencies are quoted in euros. Deviation represents standard deviation of monthly values. The full sample is 1992–2005 inclusive with the pre-euro sample encompassing 1992–1998 and the post-euro period encompassing 1999–2005.

Case 30
Young & Co.
Maeve McCutcheon, University College Cork

Howard Young gazed down from his third floor office at number 17 Parnell Mews. The next morning would see the last board meeting of the company at its current premises. This was the dawn of a new era for the company and Howard believed that the future was bright. All manner of exciting opportunities now awaited the company since its recent painful re-organisation; the problem was how best to position the company to meet those challenges. Howard knew that the board of directors was divided on the issue and the non-executive directors would be looking to him to show strong leadership. The trouble was he was still uncertain himself about the best path to take.

Background

Young & Co was founded in 1880 by Arthur H. Young, a native of Yorkshire who came to Dublin to marry the wealthy Bessie Kingston. Arthur, an engineer, brought with him a printing machine and set up in business in the coach house of his wife's family home off Parnell Square. Bessie was a leading light in the Dublin literary and musical scene, and Arthur secured the business for concert programmes, literary pamphlets poetry collections etc. It was the couple's son Gregory who really set the business on the path to growth. In the early twentieth century he spotted a niche in the production and sale of educational books. As the education system grew so the company prospered until 'Youngs' became the principal publisher of Irish produced educational texts for all levels from primary through to University texts. The company retained connections with the North of England and undertook significant contract work for Barrington's a major publisher and printer in the North East.

Edward Young brought the company to the Irish Stock Market 45 years ago. The Young family retained 20% of the shares in the company and retained a strong influence on the board of directors. Howard Young acquired the family shares and took over as managing director. Under his stewardship the company completely overhauled its printing processes and developed a state of the art printing centre in County Westmeath. The re-structuring which commenced in 2XX1 had only just been concluded. Up to this the company had operated entirely from the Parnell Square premises in Dublin city centre.

The Restructuring

'Young's' had an established reputation in Dublin as model employers, second only to the Guinness family. Moving out of Dublin had been a difficult move for the company with its Liffeyside tradition. The finance director, Lance Payne, had persuaded Howard that the company could no longer compete given its current cost base. The workforce of 140 skilled workers needed to be drastically reduced. In addition, new digital printing systems meant that the company was finding it difficult to compete on quality unless it significantly re-tooled. The subsequent negotiations with the trade unions were difficult and protracted. Generous redundancy packages were paid. In 2XX3 an employee share ownership trust, funded entirely by the company vested 5% of the issued share capital in the employees. David Little, the union representative, now had a seat on the board of directors.

The re-structuring, which was completed in 2XX5, cost the company €10 million, of which €6.5 million represented the capital costs of acquiring and re-furbishing the new premises, and €3.5 million represented redundancy and other payments to employees. The company's reserves were rapidly depleted especially as the board decided to maintain the dividend at the 2XX1 level of 22c per share. The company had one million shares in issue. The re-structuring was financed by a €10 million loan secured by a first charge on the Parnell Square premises. The loan on an interest only basis was at 6% variable rate for a ten year term with an early repayment option. Based on a recent valuation the premises and adjoining lands, all of which were zoned residential, had been valued at €20million. The company had shied away from debt in the past, preferring to grow organically, and the only other borrowing was an overdraft facility.

Market Sentiment

Howard was disappointed at the company's recent share price performance. While the restructuring had been generally welcomed when it was announced in 2XX1, the company's share price, which had advanced form €18 to €23 at that time, had generally hovered around €24 since then. In 2XX5 the company had one million shares in issue which gave a total value for the company of €34 million, effectively valuing the core business at only €14 million. Howard was sure that the market was ignoring 'Young's' growth potential. Returns on equity have been around 10% representing an equity risk premium of 5%. The company's traditional business has an un-levered beta of one, but the multimedia aspect which currently accounted for 10% of revenue, has an un-levered beta of 1.5. The traditional business was expected to grow at 2%, but a rate of 10% was not unreasonable for the multimedia business for the foreseeable future. A re-investment rate of about 15% would be needed in both areas.

The company had recorded losses in the years 2XX1 to 2XX3, but had returned to profitability in 2XX4. Its 2XX5 results had not yet been posted, but were broadly in line with market expectations (see Appendix 1). While no tax had been paid in recent years due to the losses sustained, the company can expect to pay tax at 12.5% in 2XX6.

A Growth Strategy

Brad Masters, a native of San Jose California, joined the company in 2XX3. Brad, who was married to Howard's sister Helga, had cashed out of his software business just before the dot.com collapse. He was impressed by the high level of technical expertise in 'Young's' staff and was interested in working with a small group of employees to develop new educational software packages. 'This is a worldwide market,' he enthused 'and you've got the network to really cash in. You won't grow the traditional business at more than 2 to 3%. We should re-orientate towards this growth area. Sure it's risky but we have a lot of strengths in this area.'

Brad believes that the way forward for the company is through a management buyout of the core business. They could buy the entire company having arranged to sell the Dublin premises for €20 million. They would then pay down all the existing debt. He was ready to commit €5 million and, through his connections in the venture capital community, was confident he could readily raise the balance needed in high yield debt finance at around 9%. 'We could take the company private at €28 per share.' reasoned Brad. 'We really don't need the listing and the buyout will bring back control of the company to the family. When we have this puppy turned around we can go back to the market and make a killing.'

Conserving the Assets

Lance Payne, the finance director, has little time for Brad's growth ambitions. He believes that the company now needs a period of consolidation. He has secured a tenant for the Parnell Square premises who is willing to enter into a ten year lease at €500,000 per year. Given the amount of re-fitting involved they were unlikely to be able to negotiate a shorter lease. 'Rental Yields are not really reflecting current property values,' he admitted 'especially as ten year fixed rate is currently 8%. That said, this level of lease would remove most of the financial risk from the borrowing and leave the company with a nice investment going forward. I read a report which said that property prices should continue to grow by 10% per annum for the future. Suppose we sell in year 11, we would be looking at 11 years of cumulative growth at 10% even after costs. We would still be diversified into property, which should please the shareholders and with the increased income we could afford to increase our dividend to 75 cents for the future and still leave a nice little surplus for a rainy day.'

Distributing the Gains

David Little is pressing for the immediate sale of the premises. He favours a special dividend, as dividends paid to the employee share ownership trust would be tax exempt. He reasons that with the borrowing repaid, the company could pay a special dividend of €10 per share and a regular dividend of €1 per share. 'The union has delivered on the re-structuring,' he declared 'and deserve an immediate return. We should sell the premises, repay the borrowing and return the surplus to the shareholders. This would remove the burden of debt from the shoulders of the company and allow us all to earn higher returns in the future.'

Evaluating the Choices

Howard could see problems with each course of action. He was excited by the prospects in educational software and multimedia products and agreed that that should be the target growth area. While a buyout made sense with undervalued stock, what would happen if it didn't succeed? He was unsure about how much the core business was really worth without the Dublin premises. Howard was also concerned about the amount of debt involved. Traditionally 'Young's' had been debt free and he was not convinced that they should commit to future borrowing. He might consider increasing his own investment in the business if necessary.

In relation to the lease option, he was not sure that his usually cautious finance director had a real feel for the property market. He did not seem to realise the risks involved and it was a pity to keep the capital tied up in this way. Where is the return on this investment? From his experience, a property investment of this kind with 50% debt financing should be giving a return of 12%

In relation to the sale of the premises, he had little sympathy for David's views, as he felt that the workers had already been well compensated. Taking €10 million out of the company in a special dividend was tantamount to admitting the company had no investment options. A share re-purchase might well be a better option, but Howard was aware that if his holding went above 30% he would need to make an offer for the remainder of the equity. Also, would the company not be better served with at least some borrowing?

'Questions, questions, questions.' thought Howard. 'What I really need are some answers.'

Required

You are an independent consultant employed by Howard to write a confidential report evaluating each of the options currently being explored by Young & Co. In particular your report should address the following:

Question 1

With respect to the management buyout strategy:

(a) An analysis of the buyout option. This should include consideration of the value of the core business, the financing requirements for the buyout and the ownership structure post buyout. You may assume that Howard and the employee share ownership trust retain their current shareholding.

(30 marks)

(b) An assessment of how the buyout option would affect Howard personally you should include consideration of any adjustments he might wish to make to the buyout proposal and of the circumstances in which the buyout might fail.

(15 marks)

Question 2

With respect to the property lease option:

(a) An evaluation of the lease proposal assuming Howard's cost of capital of 12% is appropriate and that the property is disposed of in year 11.

(5 marks)

(b) Assist Howard in providing an explanation to Lance as to why an investment in property could require a return of 12%, when borrowing secured on property costs 6% at present?

(10 marks)

Question 3

With respect to the special dividend, comment on the relative merits for the shareholders of a regular dividend, a special dividend and a share repurchase.

(15 marks)

Question 4

Recommend a course of action to Howard.

(25 marks)

Total 100 marks

Appendix 1
Recent Financial Results for Young & Co

€'000	2XX0	2XX1	2XX2	2XX3	2XX4	2XX5*
Gross Revenue	4450	4495	4674	4852	5012	5162
Operating Costs	3560	3371	3272	2911	2757	2839
Gross Profit	890	1,124	1,402	1,941	2,255	2323
SG&A	356	360	374	388	401	413
Depreciation	167	282	246	243	209	226
EBIT	367.0	482.1	782.3	1309.6	1645.4	1684
Interest	26	632	618	645	609	610
Extraordinary	0	200	400	2000	900	100
Tax						
Net Profit	341.0	-349.9	-235.7	-1335.4	136.4	974
Dividends	209	209	220	220	220	**

* Not yet published
** Not yet finalised

Case 31

The Good-to-Go Food Company

Maeve McCutcheon, University College Cork

Overview of the Company

Sam Hall slowly closed the file on the Good-to-Go (GTG) business plan. 'Its certainly got potential,' he mused 'but what are they teaching them in business school these days.' Sam a business mentor with the South Western Angel Network (SWAN) had a reputation for picking winners and his opinion was respected among the venture capital community. A project endorsed by Sam would always get serious consideration. Sam had established a very successful range of coffee bars in the early nineties at a time when no-one would have envisaged that the Irish would be queuing at 7:30 a.m. to drink coffee outdoors out of paper cups. Having sold out his chain to an American multinational eager to get a foothold in the Irish market he was now working full time assisting companies to the first step on the ladder.

He first met Ted Foster (aged 31) and Ross Grant (aged 29) the prime movers behind the Good-to-Go business plan three weeks ago when they had outlined their concept for healthy food options designed for the school lunch trade. Ted is a marketing major who worked all his life in his family's restaurant business while Ross is a process engineer with a passion for food. The two have been friends since college and always had the dream of starting their own business. They recognised a gap in the market for healthy-food dispensers suitable for installation in schools and clubs. The growing concern about teenage obesity was leading many schools to abandon traditional soft drinks and food dispensers yet a lot did not have the space or manpower to sell food directly to the students.

Ted and Ross had each given up their full time jobs nine months ago to focus on getting the business off the ground. Ted had borrowed €100,000 from his father while Ross had a personal loan secured on his home for €100,000. The two worked full time out of Ross's garage and used the kitchens of Ted's family restaurant for food development. They were lucky to have secured the help of Ted's cousin Mick, a full time chef in the development stage. Ted and Ross estimated that Mick had already contributed €50,000 in sweat equity. Ross had worked for Henchard's Engineering which produced refrigeration and dispensing equipment. He had persuaded David Henchard the managing director to manufacture a prototype of his design which would store and dispense 100 food products and drinks.

Ted and Ross saw themselves as men with a mission. Having been bullied in school because of his size Ted was well aware of the difficulties in adopting healthy eating practices. 'Look Sam' he had said when they met previously 'the products have to taste really good. Most health snacks taste like...well they taste pretty bad. Being healthy isn't enough when you can sneak out to the chipper on the corner. We've put a lot of time into designing a menu of pitta breads, wraps and bagels that taste as good as they are, and delicious fruit smoothies and juices that have to be nicer than a can of Coke.'

'The real challenge,' added Ross 'is to get the food to the customer tasting the way it tastes when it's assembled. We are not interested in selling the kind of soggy product on sale in corner shops which tastes strongly of the wrapper and little else. We have put a lot of thought into our packaging and we will stock the dispensers daily and clearly label each product by date.'

Getting the Show on the Road

The first GTG food dispenser was installed in the Ballymount Girls' School, a large State secondary school with 1,000 pupils located just one mile from Ted's family restaurant. Ted, who had the reputation of being persuasive, found that Miss Waters the Principal drove a hard bargain: 'Five percent of revenue to cope with the cleaning costs. You supply two large bins which you empty daily. No access to the school between nine and three and I must personally approve any product changes. Have you insurance?'

The experience with the prototype was encouraging. After three weeks in operation the dispenser was sold out at 'first break' and Miss Waters eventually agreed to three dispensers. The two friends were very encouraged with this result. Teething problems with the dispensers had been quickly resolved. With a potential target population of 500,000 in the 10 to 18 year age group they reasoned that there is a market for at least 1,500 dispensers.

Ross had prepared an initial costing of the product based on a price of €2. Their market research indicated that €2 was a significant cut-off point. Although most days the dispensers were fully cleared out, they felt it prudent to estimate an 80% sales rate. They had also factored in the short school year which is only 30 weeks long (having allowed for mid terms and break days). On this basis they estimated a gross profit per dispenser of €8,100 (see Appendix 1).

Plans for Growth

Competition in the snack market is intense and the friends agreed that it would be important to scale up quickly to get first mover advantage and go for rapid market penetration. They felt they could comfortably operate the business within the greater Dublin area, but were interested in franchising throughout the country. Under the franchise arrangement the franchisees would purchase the dispensers.

GTG would be responsible for all advertising etc, and would supply all packaging at cost. The franchise agreement would be an annual fee of €4,500 per year with a review after five years. Ross estimated that the cost to them of servicing the franchisees would be in the region of €500.

Henchards had quoted a price of €25,000 per dispenser to include a ten year maintenance contract. The dispenser would have an expected useful life of ten years. Ross reasoned that Henchards could produce up to 300 dispensers per year. New dispensers would be purchased and installed during the summer months and in this way, a full year's revenue would be available in the year of installation. If they got the dispensers up and running in Dublin first they would have a demonstrably good product to sell on to franchisees. By year six they planned to have 1,500 GTG dispensers operating throughout the country with 800 being owned and 700 being franchised (see Appendix 2).

Growth beyond the initial start-up period was more difficult to predict. It was evident to Sam that Ross and Ted were not agreed on a longer term strategy. Ted favoured expanding the product range and targeting the 20 to 30 age range with higher value added products. Ross had doubts about the amount that anyone would be willing to pay for food from a dispenser, no matter how tasty or well presented. He favoured ultimately expanding the franchise operation to the UK.

Looking for Money

Ted and Ross hoped to maintain control of the business and to allow Mike to participate as well. They had decided that their salaries should be dependent on growth in the business and that they should take out €1,000 per machine which they would split 40% each and 20% to Mike. They were surprised when their initial projections showed the business to be profitable in the first year, before allowing for financing costs (see Appendix 3).

They had made tentative approaches to the small business unit of their local bank but were unhappy at the response. The bank offered them 10% variable rate on a €1 million loan secured by personal guarantees with principal repayments of €250,000 per year, commencing in year three. The annual interest would be charged on the opening balance and there would be no early repayment option. There would still be a significant shortfall from the capital required to start the business on the rapid growth trajectory envisaged by its founders.

Sam felt that a venture capitalist (VC) could accept a year six valuation at ten times earnings before interest, taxes, depreciation and amortisation (EBITDA). The funding would be convertible preference shares with a 10% cumulative preference dividend. In addition to the preference dividend, the VC would require the conversion rights in year six to give a 35% internal rate of return on the money advanced. For the VCs to advance the money they would need to be persuaded that the founders had a viable plan beyond year six.

Sam called in Daisy May his trusted assistant analyst. 'Look,' he said 'these figures just don't stack up. They are going to have to adjust their expectations. We expect entrepreneurs to be optimistic but they need a reality check. Also, how am

I going to sell those salaries to a VC? I'll be meeting these guys next week send them out a report on their plan that brings them a bit closer to this planet'

Required

You are Daisy May; prepare a report for Ted and Ross on the feasibility of their business plan. Your report should highlight the following:

Question 1
Based on the business plan supplied by Ted and Ross you should identify:

(a) The implications of their plan for the total financing needs of the business over the six year period. Comment as appropriate.

(10 marks)

(b) The terms under which the finance would be supplied by a venture capitalist. This should include details of the equity stake sought by the venture capitalist and the amount and timing of the preference dividends together with any other condition which a venture capitalist is likely to impose.

(25 marks)

Question 2
Produce a revised business plan in which you:

(a) Review the salary payments to Ted, Ross and Mike, and explain the need for any adjustments you propose.

(10 marks)

(b) Revise the growth schedule with the objective of achieving full implementation by year six while retaining control.

(25 marks)

Question 3
Compare the terms of the bank financing and the venture capital financing focussing on:

(a) A comparison of cost and risk of each form of financing.

(15 marks)

(b) A consideration of the broader impact of venture capital involvement on a growth business.

(15 marks)

Total 100 marks

Appendix 1
Estimate of Revenue per Dispenser

GTG Dispenser

Capacity	100 units
Usage 80%	80 units
Annual Sales Based on 150 days	12,000 units
Gross revenue €2 per item	€24,000
Cost of sales	€14,400
Net revenue	€9,600
Distribution	€1,500
Earnings per dispenser	€8,100

Appendix 2
Projected Installation Schedule for GTG Dispensers

	Year 1	Year 2	Year 3	Year 4	Year 5	Year 6
Machines	200	500	800	1100	1300	1500
Franchise			200	400	600	700
Company owned	200	500	600	700	700	800

Appendix 3
Earnings Projections

	Year 1 €	Year 2 €	Year 3 €	Year 4 €	Year 5 €	Year 6 €
Gross revenue	4,800,000	12,000,000	14,400,000	16,800,000	16,800,000	19,200,000
Franchise income	0	0	800,000	1,600,000	2,400,000	2,800,000
Revenue	4,800,000	12,000,000	15,200,000	18,400,000	19,200,000	22,000,000
Cost of sales	2,880,000	7,200,000	8,640,000	10,080,000	10,080,000	11,520,000
Distribution	300,000	750,000	900,000	1,050,000	1,050,000	1,200,000
Advertising	500,000	500,000	100,000	100,000	100,000	100,000
Salaries	200,000	500,000	800,000	1,100,000	1,300,000	1,500,000
EBITDA	920,000	3,050,000	4,760,000	6,070,000	6,670,000	7,680,000
Tax		115,000	381,250	595,000	758,750	833,750
Depreciation		1,250,000	2,000,000	2,750,000	3,250,000	3,750,000
Profit	920,000	1,685,000	2,378,750	2,725,000	2,661,250	3,096,250

Case 32
Plastic Products
Derry Cotter, University College Cork

Overview of the Company

Plastic Products Limited is a large private company. The company has achieved excellent profit performance since incorporation ten years ago, but in recent years the rate of annual sales growth has not been maintained. The board of directors is currently evaluating how this problem might be addressed. Two alternative strategies are being considered. The first involves internal expansion by identifying capital projects to expand the Company's existing sales level. Alternatively, Plastic Products Limited is considering a policy of expansion by means of the acquisition of other smaller companies with an established sales base.

(a) Internal Growth

A number of capital projects are currently being examined. One such project is the proposal to commence production of a new plastic component, codenamed 'the Plastech.' Details are as follows:

- Machinery, costing €400,000, would have to be purchased immediately (i.e. on 31 July 2XX6). This machinery is expected to have a useful life of four years, at which point it is expected to have a residual value of €50,000.

- Capital allowances can be claimed at 20% per annum on a straight line basis.

- Design costs will total €100,000, of which €70,000 has been paid, and a further €20,000 contracted for and payable at the end of July 2XX7.

- Sales are estimated at 60,000 units per annum for four years. The unit selling price of 'the Plastech' will be €10 per unit.

- The unit contribution margin, before deducting depreciation on new machinery, and before deducting bad debts and discount, is expected to be 50%.

- Fixed overheads will be €150,000 per annum. This includes €30,000 of head office management charges.

- Stocks of 'the Plastech' of 10% of the following year's sales volume are required. It should be assumed that stocks are valued on the basis of unit variable cost.
- Customers will receive three months credit on sales, and bad debts are estimated at 3% of sales. Alternatively, the offer of a cash discount of 2% for payment within one month would reduce bad debts to 1% of total sales. It is expected that 60% of customers would take up the offer of the cash discount.
- Plastic Products Limited will receive one month's credit from its raw material supplier. Raw materials represent 40% of total variable costs.
- Annual interest at 12% will be incurred in financing working capital requirements. Initial working capital requirements should be assumed to arise on 31 July 2XX6.
- Should this project be undertaken, an immediate saving of €60,000 redundancy costs will be made, and machinery which would otherwise have had to be scrapped at an immediate cost of €20,000 will now be utilised.

Sources of Finance

Plastic Products Limited has one million issued equity shares, with an estimated market value of €50 per share (ex-div). Additional equity capital would be issued at a discount of 10% and issue expenses would amount to €3 per share.

Plastic Products Limited has a constant dividend payout ratio of 30% of after tax profits.

Profits after tax in recent years have been as follows:

2XX1	€1,100,000
2XX2	€1,400,000
2XX3	€900,000
2XX4	€1,500,000
2XX5	€1,850,000

The company also has €15 million of 7% irredeemable preference shares. The estimated market value is €108 per €100 nominal and half a year's dividend is accrued.

Plastic Products Limited also has €10 million of 10% irredeemable debentures. The current market value is €118, including one year's accrued interest.

Leasing

Should Plastic Products Limited decide to proceed with the 'Plastech' project, the machinery required on 31 July can be acquired by outright purchase, or alternatively it can be leased. Four lease instalments of €130,000 would be payable annually in advance. Plastic Products Limited has access to borrowed funds at a rate of 10%. If the new machine is leased, possession of the machine will revert to the lessor at the end of 2XX9.

(b) External Growth

As part of its alternative expansion route of 'growth by acquisition', Plastic Products Limited is currently examining the possible purchase of a small local company. Metal Fasteners Limited was founded in June 2XX1 by George Simpson, who is now considering selling the Company, with a view to exploring other interests. A listed company engaged in the same sector of the metal industry had earnings of €10 million for the most recent financial year (forecast earnings for 2XX6 of €15 million). This company's share price was €2 per share when its results were released, and it has 50 million issued equity shares. Its P/E ratio has not changed significantly over the years. An analysis of its financial position shows that Metal Fasteners Limited has a substantially higher debt equity ratio than the industry norm. This differential largely relates to a long term loan of €500,000 raised by Metal Fasteners Limited on 1 December 2XX5, at a fixed rate of interest of 10% per annum.

The accounting policies used by Metal Fasteners Limited are typical of the metal industry, but the application of the accounting policies of Plastic Products Limited would increase annual after tax earnings by €30,000. Should Plastic Products Limited decide to acquire Metal Fasteners Limited, once-off rationalisation costs of €200,000 will be incurred, but annual synergy benefits of €150,000 will be achieved. Plastic Products Limited will also be able to dispose of part of the premises of Metal Fasteners Limited for €480,000. This asset has a net book value of €180,000 and has been depreciated at 2% per annum on a reducing balance basis. The market value of the other land and buildings is €1.3 million.

A summary of financial information relating to Metal Fasteners Limited is outlined in Appendix 1.

(c) Additional Information

The following information should be assumed to apply in respect of Plastic Products Limited:

(i) The company pays corporation tax at 40%, one year in arrears
(ii) The accounting year end is 31 July

The following information should be assumed to apply in respect of Metal Fasteners Limited:

(i) The company pays corporation tax at 40%
(ii) The company does not have any losses forward

Required

As finance director of Plastic Products Limited, you are required to prepare a report for the board of directors relating to the Company's desire to achieve increased growth in its level of sales. Your report should specifically address the following issues:

1. Internal expansion

In respect of the proposed 'Plastech' project you are required to undertake the following analysis-

(a) Calculate the payback period, based on the net cash outflow at 31 July 2XX6.

(3 marks)

(b) Calculate the accounting rate of return.

(5 marks)

(c) Calculate Plastic Products Limited's weighted average cost of capital.

(10 marks)

(d) Recommend whether this project should be accepted should the internal expansion route be adopted.

(20 marks)

(e) Measure the extent to which the outcome of the project is sensitive to the level of fixed overheads.

(5 marks)

(f) Evaluate the alternative methods of financing the acquisition of the machinery on 31 July 2XX6.

(7 marks)

2. External growth

In respect of the proposed acquisition of Metal Fasteners Limited, you are required to prepare the following information:

(a) A valuation of Metal Fasteners Limited using both an assets and an earnings basis.

(20 marks)

(b) A recommendation as to what value would be considered appropriate, and the optimal manner in which the consideration package should be structured.

(9 marks)

(c) An evaluation of the alternative methods of financing the proposed acquisition.

(6 marks)

(d) A discussion of the current dividend policy of Plastic Products Limited in the light of the possible flotation of its shares.

(9 marks)

(e) An examination of the alternatives available to Plastic Products Limited to address the risk of an interest rate increase, should the acquisition of Metal Fasteners Limited be financed by borrowings.

(6 marks)

Total 100 marks

Appendix 1
Balance Sheet of Metal Fasteners Limited at 31 December 2XX5

	€'000	€'000
Fixed assets		
Land and buildings	1,100	
Plant and machinery	950	
Fixtures and fittings	200	
		2,250
Current assets		
Stocks	900	
Debtors	1,300	
Bank	150	
	2,350	
Current liabilities		
Creditors	800	
Dividend proposed	100	
Taxation	724	
Working capital		726
Net assets		2,976
Financed by;		
Ordinary share capital		100
Revenue reserves		1,376
Ordinary shareholders' funds		1,476
Loans		1,500
		2,976

> **Appendix 1 (continued)**

Profit and Loss A/C of Metal Fasteners Limited for the Year Ended 31st December 2XX5

	€'000
Turnover	3,900
Cost of sales	(1,600)
Gross profit	2,300
Net operating expenses	(800)
Foreign exchange loss	(50)
Profit on ordinary activities before interest	1,450
Interest	(170)
Profit on ordinary activities before taxation	1,280
Taxation	(400)
Profit for financial year	880
Dividends	(100)
Retained profit for the financial year	780
Revenue reserves at 1st January 2XX5	596
Revenue reserves at 31 December 2XX5	1,376

Should Plastic Products Limited proceed with the acquisition of Metal Fasteners Limited there are different views as to how the purchase should be financed. The Board would prefer to fund the acquisition with further debt, but there has been speculation that the Company's Bankers would apply restrictive covenants, and that Plastic Products Limited may not have appropriate security for the loan required. There is also concern that a substantial interest rate increase will arise prior to the required funds being drawn down by Plastic Products Limited.

As an alternative the board is considering a flotation of the Company's shares on the Alternative Investment Market. They are reluctant to adopt this latter course of action however, as Plastic Products Limited uses income decreasing policies (relative to quoted companies in the plastics industry). It is feared that this would result in the Company's shares being quoted at a discount.

Case 33
Homemade Pies plc
John Cotter, University College Dublin

Overview of the Company

Homemade Pies is a specialist food producing company located in Co. Tyrone in the heart of mid-Ulster. The number of employees in the company has been reasonably constant with 102 being on the books over the previous year. It has a great reputation for producing quality food products, and, in particular, its handmade pies have won numerous national and international food awards. Traditionally, the company exported its products, with very profitable markets in many wealthy economies, including the US and Japan. Domestically, it was seen as a leader in producing high quality food specialist products, although this market was fairly small. However, this domestic market was very profitable and has been developing quite rapidly in recent years. The finance director of the company, Mr. James Lowe, believes that company has reached its 'steady state' in terms of profitability and can continue to employ this number of staff for the foreseeable future.

Discussion of Pension

Homemade Pies has always been seen as an attractive employer in the local economy. A number of reasons have been cited including the personal benefits bestowed on all staff. For instance, it was always progressive in providing pension contributions to its employees and it has a long running defined contribution scheme operating for all members. This defined contribution scheme calculates the benefits accruing to employees based on the value of the fund when an employee retires. Details of the current assets and liabilities of the scheme are provided in Appendix 1.

The finance director has prime responsibility for the operation and management of the pension scheme. In his role, he has required outside advice on a number of issues but only followed policies that he was supportive of. He has always felt that the investment strategy of the pension funds should be mixed across a set of asset types such as equities and property. He also recognised that these assets can incur high levels of risk that may not benefit the pension investment fund, so has also included relatively 'safe' fixed income type assets.

The total fund is in many different assets including: technology stocks, airline stock and financial stocks for equities; government gilts – five year and 20 year; commercial paper; time based deposits for fixed income assets and both commercial and retail property. The only investment rules governing the fund is the make-up of the portfolio of 50% equities, 30% fixed income and 20% property, and no investment is allowed in agricultural or related assets. He knew from experience that equities have the potential of being very risky, with a lot of downside price performance, and wanted to ensure that the pension investment fund diversified away from the core industry of Homemade Pies. Similar performances were recorded for Homemade Pies pension assets in 2XX1 and 2XX2 (falling by 10% each year). However, the fund performed very well in 2XX0 with a return of 26%, and since 2XX2 has achieved positive, if erratic, returns with an average of 8% per annum.

The liabilities of the fund are based on potential pension contributions for Homemade Pies, with advice been given by a consultancy firm that specialises in the investments and also in the pensions area. The calculation is based on having an average pensionable number of employees of 100 with an average retirement lifetime of ten years per person. Also the average contributions are €25,000 per annum. Thus the total calculated liabilities are calculated as the No Employees * No years of scheme*contributions: 100*10*25k = €25 million. Although the finance director has expressed confidence in the future performance of the company and the numbers employed, he has also suggested that an average pension payment of €25,000 is reasonable given the salary packages offered by the firm and others in the industry. However, he has not done any sensitivity analysis on the average number of years a pension member would receive payments from their retirement.

Part B of Appendix 1 details the expected return and risk performance of the assets of the pension scheme on a yearly basis. These are predicted estimates obtained from their consultancy findings. The report suggests that while fixed income investments offer low returns, they also are very safe with low expected deviation. The report uses the capital asset pricing model (CAPM) to discuss the relative merits of the assets chosen and the predicted returns and risk estimates are obtained from Ibbotson and Co that estimates expected returns and risk based on past performance of assets using data from over 100 years.

Defined Benefit Pensions

As stated, Homemade Pies (plc) have a defined contribution scheme in place that pays according to the value of the fund when an employee retires. However, there are other pension funds open to the company, in defined benefit schemes, and the finance director is interested in examining the merits of these. Defined benefit schemes calculate the benefit according to factors such as final salary, length of pensionable service and the age of the member. The payments are made regardless of the value of a company's pension investment fund at the time of an employee retirement. If there is a deficit between the company's pension assets and its liabilities in the form of pension contributions, there is a government backed scheme to support these pension schemes.

Note on Pension Protection Funds and Homemade Pies

The finance director, James Lowe, has done some research on the current pension provision in the UK detailing current legislation, current schemes and their operations. He provides the following information. A new scheme, the Pension Protection Fund (PPF) was introduced in the UK as a result of the Pensions Act 2004. The idea behind the legislation was to help many pensions that faced financial difficulties as a result of poor investment performance and, specifically, to ensure that these pensions were returned to full funding, that is, the assets of the pension met the required liability contributions. Prior to the legislation many defined pension schemes were severely underfunded (and some insolvent) leading to a crises in financially supporting the retirement of many participating employees. The new system for defined benefit pension schemes, the PPF, has the following key functions: First, the PPF is required to pay compensation to members of eligible defined benefit pension schemes, when there is a qualifying insolvency event (defined as liabilities exceeding assets) in relation to the sponsor (company with defined benefit pension scheme). Second the PPF receives its funds for compensation purposes by way of imposing compulsory levies on all eligible member schemes and it is this function that we are going to concentrate our discussions (for comprehensive information on the levies and the scheme in general see Blake et al, 2006).

The rational for the development of the PPF from the UK government's perspective was to ensure that a guarantee system was in place so that employees and employers knew with certainty that full pension rights were guaranteed. Also the system should ensure that taxpayers are not required to bail out the system by providing financial support to ensure employees got their full future benefits. Essentially, the smooth operation of the PPF would require that the contributions (levies) imposed on defined benefit pension schemes be sufficient to meet future pension underfunding. For instance, speaking at the Labour Party annual conference on 1 October 2003, the Chancellor of the Exchequer Gordon Brown said the government will 'legislate for a new statutory pension protection fund. In future every worker contributing to a pension will have their pension protected and be guaranteed their pension rights.' This means that a promise made by a scheme sponsor to pay a certain pension is being guaranteed by the PPF.

Further details of the PPF are also provided. The PPF has a set of rules that are to be followed for defined benefit pension schemes. First, for each defined benefit pension scheme they have to pay a yearly levy. The fee from joining the PPF involved yearly levies charged with a cap of 0.5% of the sponsoring company's pension fund liabilities. The actual levy is set on a specific date e.g. March 31, and will not be required to be added to over the year following this date. Homemade Pies (and other sponsoring companies) may be able to manipulate the size of the levy required at this time by ensuring that their asset values are maximised and liabilities minimised at the time that the levy is introduced thereby reducing the cost of being protected by the scheme.

Second, for the pension scheme to receive financial support from the PPF it has to meet the criteria for entry into the scheme, namely, that the sponsoring employer has a pension scheme that has become insolvent with no chance of recovery. Third, once insolvency is established, the PPF takes responsibility for the member scheme and once in, the scheme will remain the responsibility of the PPF. There is a suggestion that this type of scheme may induce some undesirable behaviour amongst sponsors of defined benefit pension schemes. For instance, the scheme might allow participants to exhibit 'moral hazard,' that is they change their behaviour after joining the pension fund relative to before joining the scheme. Also the fact that the PPF will guarantee pension rights for member schemes might encourage sponsoring firms to become members by underfunding their pension schemes in advance of bankruptcy (and thereby use the funds for some other non-pension related activities of the business). Also the PPF has no authority to dictate the types of assets members are allowed to invest in for developing their pension funds, although they would like members to show prudence in their investment strategy.

After paying the levy, the member scheme (once meeting the insolvency criteria) is eligible to receive financial support from the PPF. The PPF offers two types of compensation for defined benefit schemes of relevance to Homemade Pies. The PPF protects 100% of the pension for members above scheme pension age or already in receipt of a pension due to ill health or it being a survivor's pension (its previous employees), and 90% of the promised pension for the remaining members below scheme pension age (its current employees) up to a maximum of €25,000.

Required

You have been asked to act as an independent consultant to advise Homemade Pies on the best way to deal with their pension requirements. A number of issues should be dealt with in your report:

Question 1
You are asked to assess the current value of the assets and liabilities of Homemade Pies pension funds. Treating the pension assets and liabilities separately from the remaining assets and liabilities of the firm, calculate the working capital of the pension fund of the company. Also show, using ratios, (e.g. current ratio etc) the viability of the company's pension fund. Explain all assumptions that you make.

(20 marks)

Question 2
Repeat the analysis of Question 1 for the future value of the assets and liabilities of the Homemade Pies pension fund. In particular you should comment on the

assumptions relating to age of pension scheme, the discount factor used and the expected returns and risk of the assets.

(20 marks)

Question 3

Further illustrate your analysis by commenting on potential changing of the values relating to your answer in Question 1 (e.g. discount factor). Confine your comments to the estimation of the present value of the fund (no calculations are necessary for this question). Comment on the likely impact of the new results of Question 1 and how it would affect Homemade Pies in the actions they could follow in restructuring their pension plans.

(10 marks)

Question 4

Discuss the composition of the Homemade Pies pension's assets in terms of the capital asset pricing model and the views of the finance director, for example on diversification away from Agricultural investments or related assets.

(20 marks)

Question 5

Assess the relative merits of joining the Pension Protection Fund. You should discuss the current defined contribution scheme and detail how a defined benefit scheme differs from this. Also you should suggest the best solution that the company could achieve before joining the Pension Protection Fund. You should also suggest the best solution that the company could achieve after joining the Pension Protection Fund.

(30 marks)

Total 100 marks

References:
Blake, David; Cotter, John and Kevin Dowd, (2006), The Pension Protection Fund, Centre for Financial Markets, University College Dublin.
Ibbotson and Co (2005), Asset performance yearbook, Ibbotson and Co.

Appendix 1:
Details of Homemade Pies (plc) Defined Contribution Pension for year XXXX

Part A: Pension budget €(m)

Assets
Equities 5
Fixed Income 3
Property 2
Total Assets 10

Liabilities
No employees 100
No years of scheme 10
Contribution 25
Total liabilities 25

Part B: Expected performance of assets

	Returns (%)	Risk (%)
Equities	20	30
Fixed income	3	0.5
Property	20	12

Notes: There are two parts to Appendix 1. Part A details the assets and liabilities of the pension plan. The assets are based on their current market values, whereas the liabilities are based on their expected future requirements. Three types of assets are invested in. The liabilities of the pension scheme is calculated as the No Employees * No years of scheme*contributions. Further details of the estimates are given in the text. Part B details the expected return and risk annualised performance of the assets of the pension scheme.

Case 34
Mega Meals Limited
Paul McDonnell and Donal McKillop,
Queen's University Belfast

Overview of the Company

The Belfast-based business 'Mega Meals Limited' began life ten years ago in the form of a partnership between Peter Penney, an accomplished (if unqualified) chef, and his elder brother, James. In the early days, Peter travelled around surrounding fairs, markets and sporting events cooking and selling burgers, hotdogs and chips from his van. His brother James, a solicitor, contributed the funds to purchase the van and initial stock but acted as a silent partner, with a 50% share in the business.

The business was a reasonable success, generating a fair income for Peter and a good return on James' investment, but, as time progressed, Peter became increasingly disillusioned with the standard of food the company was providing, together with his peripatetic working lifestyle. Therefore, with James' consent, he employed a member of staff to run the mobile food van, while he began, using his culinary expertise, to offer high quality outside catering services. The primary events Peter provided food for were local social functions, such as funerals and weddings. Peter met Eddie Banks, the chief executive of FIFO, a Northern Ireland-wide chain of convenience stores, at the marriage of Mr Bank's daughter. Eddie was impressed by the calibre of Peter's food and asked him if he would be interested in providing a range of convenience meals and desserts, based on Peter's recipes, for sale on a trial basis in two of the FIFO's stores. Despite Peter's misgivings about the general quality of such products and his ability to maintain his high standards as the number of meals produced increased, following discussions with James, it was agreed that the FIFO proposal should be accepted.

The trial agreed upon turned out to be very successful, to the extent that Eddie Banks asked if Peter could supply a larger range of his products to be sold throughout the FIFO chain. To do this, investment in a new expanded cooking and packaging facility would be required. At this point, the Penney brothers agreed to incorporate the business as Mega Meals Limited, with both owning half of the total equity. Peter would act as the managing director, while James would contribute the €400,000 required to build the new facility and meet the initial costs of hiring new staff from his savings. Although nominally a director of the new company, James' role would remain a silent one with respect to the entity's operations.

As in the case of the trial run, Mega Meals' food proved to be extremely popular throughout all the FIFO stores. As Mega Meals did not have an exclusivity clause in their agreement (to provide foods only to FIFO), this success led other retailers to become interested in the products. As the facility built at the time of incorporation had a large amount of spare capacity, the brothers were happy to agree to provide a range of their products to a number of other Northern Ireland-based retail chains.

Mega Meals' success has continued until today. Recently, Peter, in conjunction with James and Mega Meals' chief accountant, has negotiated two major new deals. The first is an agreement with Sparks and Dempster, a leading UK-based supermarket chain, to provide a wide range of convenience meals and desserts. The deal includes a guarantee that Sparks and Dempster will continue to source all their convenience meals from Mega Meals for an initial period of two years, with a five year extension option if both parties are satisfied at the end of the period. In order to fulfil their obligations, Mega Meals is opening a major new facility on the outskirts of Birmingham. The initial investment required to do this is €3 million, which will be financed through debt. The returns generated through the Sparks and Dempster contract alone, should it be extended to the full seven year period, will be enough to repay the debt within three years, while meeting the interest payments and providing a return to the company; that is, the project has a positive Net Present Value (NPV). In addition, Peter is confident that Mega Meals will be able to negotiate further deals with UK-based companies.

The other deal negotiated by the company is for the supply of their products to Six-Twelve Inc., a regional chain of convenience stores based in Boston, Massachusetts. While primarily the same lines that are available in the UK will be sold, a greater emphasis will be placed upon identifiably Irish recipes. In this vein, the branding of the food will be changed to reflect the origin of the meals. Six-Twelve has agreed to supply all their stores with Mega Meals' products for a guaranteed period of three years following the recent completion of a successful trial. As with the Sparks and Dempster contract, it will be necessary for Mega Meals to invest in a new facility in the Boston area at an initial cost of one million US dollars. As before, this project has been analysed by the company's finance department and found to have a positive NPV when the loan will be paid off at the end of three years. In addition, Peter is extremely excited about the prospect of breaking into the American market and feels that, with the excellence of his recipes, they can't help but be as successful as they have been to this point in attracting and retaining customers.

While agreeing that both deals appear to be superb opportunities for Mega Meals, James, who is naturally cautious but does believe in the quality of his brother's products and his enthusiasm in leading the company to date, can't help but be slightly concerned. Mega Meals' chief accountant had recommended that both deals be financed through floating rate borrowings. James, however, is worried about the prospect of an interest rate rise, and would be happier if fixed rate finance were to be used. In addition, he is concerned that the returns from the US-based facility will be denominated in dollars, whereas the investment will be paid for in local currency. In response to James' concerns about the funding of the Birmingham facility, the chief accountant has suggested that the company could borrow at a fixed rate, which is higher than the current floating rate available, or undertake a swap with another company or financial institution (details of which are contained in Appendix 1). With respect to James' concerns about the risk of a weakening dollar, the accountant has identified an American company who would be willing to undertake a foreign currency swap with Mega Meals, thus allowing the company to borrow at a lower rate of interest than would be available directly from a US financial institution (details in Appendix 2). As a management consultant, James has asked you to advise him on the best way of funding Mega Meals' two new facilities.

Required

Your report to James should consist of two parts, (1) and (2), each of which should deal with one of the new investments.

In part (1), you should include:

(a) An evaluation of the benefits and drawbacks of using fixed or floating rate debt to fund the project
(b) An evaluation of the benefits and drawbacks of undertaking a swap, either directly with another company or with a financial intermediary. This should include a calculation of the cost of the various options (including a description of how the swap should be structured), a calculation of the value of the swap, a qualitative evaluation of the risk involved and a discussion of the 'comparative advantage' argument for undertaking swaps (relevant information is provided in Appendix 1)
(c) Your recommendation as to the funding of the Birmingham-based facility.

In part (2), you should include:

(a) An evaluation of the relative merits of hedging using a foreign currency swap against other potential methods
(b) A calculation of the benefit to Mega Meals of undertaking the swap, either directly or through the financial institution (details included in Appendix 2)
(c) An evaluation of the risk involved in undertaking the swap, particularly with regard to the credit risk related to Widgets Inc, the identified counterparty (you should decompose the swap into a series of forward contracts to help explain your answer)
(d) A recommendation as to how the US-based facility should be funded.

(Approximately 50 marks will be allocated to each question, with 40% of the total marks being awarded for calculations and 60% for the discussion and recommendations in both cases.)

Total 100 marks

Appendix 1
Data Supplied by Mega Meals' Accountant with Respect to its Borrowing Rates and Potential Interest Rate Swap Opportunities

	Fixed Rate (3 years)	Floating Rate (6 months)
Mega Meals	9.0%	LIBOR+2%
Cyco	7.0%	LIBOR+1%

Cyco Limited is a London-based firm which manufactures bicycles. They are willing to undertake a swap with Mega Meals, sharing any benefits (in terms of interest rates) equally between the two companies. Alternatively, an AAA-rated financial intermediary has been identified that will pay LIBOR in return for a fixed rate of 6.75%. Mega Meals requires a €3 million loan for three years. Any interest payments will be semi-annual, and the current rate of (local currency) LIBOR is 5% (six-month), with the LIBOR zero curve having a flat term structure.

Appendix 2
Data Supplied by Mega Meals' Accountant with Respect to the Potential Currency Swap

	€	$US
Mega Meals	9.0%	12.0%
Widgets	7.5%	9.0%

The rates quoted are fixed rates and have been adjusted for the effect of income taxes. The current exchange rate is 1.3$US/€, with US$ six-month LIBOR being 7.0%. The US LIBOR zero curve also has a flat term structure. Mega Meals requires $1 million for three years. Widgets Inc. is happy to undertake the currency swap for the amount and period suggested, either directly or through a financial institution. The principal amounts involved are $1million and €769,231. If a direct swap is undertaken, the benefits will be shared equally between the two companies and Widgets will bear the foreign exchange risk. If a (AAA-rated) financial institution is used, its commission will be 20 basis points, and the financial institution will bear all the foreign exchange risk in the transaction.

Case 35

Genero plc

**Paul McDonnell and Donal McKillop,
Queen's University Belfast**

Overview of the Company

Genero was founded in August 2XX2 by Mike O'Reilly, in the form of a limited company. At that point, Mike had just graduated with a doctorate in biology, specialising in biological engineering. Using a loan of €50,000, provided by his parents, he set up a basic bioengineering laboratory in the basement of his house. As Mike's research had been centred on DNA synthesis, his expertise allowed him to make a major breakthrough with respect to the production of a virus that may have a commercial application in killing one specific, particularly virulent, species of weed. Following the granting of a worldwide patent on Mike's virus synthesis process, it was decided that 60% of the equity of the company should be listed on the Dublin stock exchange, (the remainder being owned by Mike and his parents), with the flotation date being 1 August 2XX3. At the end of the first day's trading, Genero plc was valued at over €15 million.

Since that point, Genero has opened a major laboratory on the outskirts of Dublin. The firm has begun work on a number of new projects and has continued to develop Mike's original patent. Although the company has yet to pay dividends (it intends to maintain this practice for at least the next two years), its share price has continued to increase since the flotation.

While the progress of Genero's stock price has been relatively steady and encouraging up until this point, the bioengineering sector in which it operates is characterised by a high degree of riskiness compared to almost every other sector of the economy. The probability of a start-up firm, such as Genero, failing in the first five years is high; however, the firms that do succeed tend to produce enormous returns for those that invest in the early stages of their existence.

Recently, Genero's investment bank, Bank of Ourland, has approached the board with a view to the listing of stock options, based on Genero, on the Eurex derivatives market. It is suggested that, initially, a range of European-style put and call options with initial times to expiry of one month, three months and twelve months should be included. The one- and three-month options would have strike prices of either €12, €12.50 or €13, while the twelve-month options exercise prices are proposed to be €12, €13 or €14, in line with EUREX regulations. In addition, it is suggested that American-style call and put options with initial time to expiry of one year (with the same strike prices as for the European options) be listed. Finally, given the high volatility of the bioengineering sector, the bank has also proposed that a number of exotic options be listed for Genero in the future. It has been mooted that these may include barrier, chooser, lookback and Asian options.

While Mike is excited about the bank's proposal, not having studied any finance or accounting, he is slightly worried that he doesn't really understand very much about it. As the company's management consultant, he has asked you to prepare a report which will enlighten him about both the nature of the proposed stock options, the methods by which they may be priced, and how factors, such as fluctuations in Genero's share price, are likely to affect the option prices in the future. Appendix 1 contains historic data relating to Genero's share price, the market index and the one-month euro treasury bill rate.

Required

Your report to Mike should include:

1. An explanation of the nature of European put and call options, including an explanation and calculation of upper/lower bounds on their prices and a discussion of put-call parity.

    (14 marks)

2. A calculation of the estimated price of the European options mentioned based on the Black-Scholes option pricing model (BSOPM), including a discussion of the assumptions used and limitations of the model, an explanation of how you estimated the volatility of the Genero share price, and an analysis of the way in which the various factors involved in the model will affect the option price.

    (20 marks)

3. A discussion of the nature of American options, including reasons why the BSOPM is not generally applicable to their valuation.

    (14 marks)

4. A valuation of the American options proposed using a binomial tree-based method, including a discussion of how and why the accuracy of the valuation changes with the number of steps in a tree.

    (14 marks)

5. An explanation of the nature of the various exotic options proposed, including a discussion of how the Monte Carlo method may be used to estimate their price.

    (14 marks)

6. A discussion of three key option price sensitivities (delta, gamma and vega).

(14 marks)

7. An evaluation of the Bank's proposal and a recommendation as to whether Genero should proceed.

(10 marks)

(You may assume that all calculations are being made in July 2XX6, the volatility of Genero's share price will remain constant over the life of the options and that the interest rate term structure is flat (i.e. the interest rate associated with a financial instrument is independent of the instrument's term to maturity). Overall, approximately 40% of the total marks will be awarded for calculations and 60% for the discussion and recommendations.

Total 100 marks

Appendix 1
Historic Data Relating to Genero's Share Price, the Market Index, and the One-Month Euro Treasury Bill Rate

Date	Genero Share Price/€	Market Index	1 month T-Bill Rate
Aug-03	2.57	3546	2.61
Sep-03	2.63	3477	2.45
Oct-03	2.91	3982	2.48
Nov-03	3.35	4952	2.44
Dec-03	3.34	4614	2.41
Jan-04	3.56	4887	2.40
Feb-04	3.84	5336	2.52
Mar-04	4.27	6184	2.50
Apr-04	4.52	6492	2.58
May-04	4.85	6976	2.52
Jun-04	5.11	7253	2.56
Jul-04	5.22	7092	2.55
Aug-04	5.50	7370	2.57
Sep-04	5.78	7614	2.64
Oct-04	5.82	7236	2.65
Nov-04	5.82	6778	2.68
Dec-04	5.86	6420	2.73
Jan-05	5.89	6087	2.71
Feb-05	5.64	5212	2.68
Mar-05	6.02	5567	2.71
Apr-05	6.62	6307	2.69
May-05	6.82	6265	2.67
Jun-05	7.10	6363	2.68
Jul-05	7.66	6930	2.64
Aug-05	7.93	6951	2.64
Sep-05	8.17	6903	2.64
Oct-05	8.37	6796	2.59
Nov-05	8.03	5860	2.61
Dec-05	8.30	5849	2.63
Jan-06	8.84	6213	2.62
Feb-06	8.40	5260	2.58
Mar-06	9.52	6318	2.57
Apr-06	9.12	5432	2.55
May-06	9.81	5887	2.55
Jun-06	10.45	6251	2.56
Jul-06	11.03	6522	2.54